Blacks who have attained responsible
positions on newspapers, magazines, radio and
TV and in the worlds of advertising and
public relations, and others just starting out,
vividly present the problems and position of
black men and women in their field today,
and their views of the future.

BLACKS IN COMMUNICATIONS
Journalism, Public Relations and Advertising

For many years, blacks in this country were virtually excluded from responsible positions on newspapers, magazines, radio and TV and in the worlds of advertising and public relations. Today, increasing numbers of blacks are playing vital roles in the communications industry—both in white-run organizations and in rapidly expanding black enterprises. In this book, blacks who have "made it" and others just starting out vividly present the problems and position of black men and women in their field today, and their views of the future.

Books by M. L. Stein

BLACKS IN COMMUNICATIONS
Journalism, Public Relations and Advertising

FREEDOM OF THE PRESS
A Continuing Struggle

UNDER FIRE
The Story of American War Correspondents

WHEN PRESIDENTS MEET THE PRESS

YOUR CAREER IN JOURNALISM

BLACKS IN COMMUNICATIONS

Journalism, Public Relations and Advertising

by M. L. STEIN

photographs

JULIAN MESSNER NEW YORK

Published by Julian Messner
a division of Simon & Schuster, Inc.
1 West 39th Street, New York, N.Y. 10018

For the AEJ summer interns, past and future

Printed in the United States of America

ISBN 0-671-32511-6 Cloth Trade
       0-671-32512-4 MCE

Library of Congress Catalog Card No. 78-182947

Contents

Acknowledgments

I am grateful to the men and women who took their valuable time to provide interviews and material for this book. Some of the persons in these pages are prominent in their fields. Others are in the early stages of their careers, and prominence doubtless awaits them. There was no attempt here to seek out only those who have achieved distinction. The object, instead, was to provide the best cross section possible of blacks in the communications media. The book is not intended as an encyclopedia of all blacks engaged in journalism. All of the men and women in this book are doing difficult jobs well, and certainly all are pioneers in occupations that previously had a "White Only" label on them.

I also want to thank certain media organizations for their contributions and cooperation in this project. Specifically, they are the Associated Press, United Press International, *The New York Times*, NBC News, ABC News, CBS News, *Redbook* magazine, the *Detroit News*, the *Chicago Tribune*, KOMO-TV, Seattle, *Ebony* magazine, *Time*, Inc., the *Washington Post*, the Memphis *Commercial Appeal*, Field Enterprises, Inc., KRON-TV, San Francisco and *Newsweek* magazine.

— M. L. Stein

1/The Way It Is Now

Shortly before this was written, the Portland *Oregonian*, a newspaper with a daily circulation of 245,000, announced that it had appointed William Arthur Hilliard as city editor. What made this more than a routine announcement was the fact that Bill Hilliard was the first black man to rise so high on a major American daily newspaper.

Hilliard, who began as an *Oregonian* copy boy in 1952, is one of a number of black newsmen and women on white or Establishment newspapers throughout the United States. In addition, blacks are represented on news magazines, press associations, broadcast stations and networks and in public relations and advertising. Some of them were hired out of liberal arts colleges and journalism schools. Others moved from jobs on black newspapers. Still others came from fields unrelated to journalism. Melba Tolliver was a secretary at the American Broadcasting Company in New York when an executive decided that she might make a good news announcer. He gave her a tryout and was impressed with her poise and surefootedness in reading the news. ABC then sent her to New York University for journalism training. When she returned, she was made a part of the ABC evening news team and has handled a number of top stories.

The author does not mean to suggest in this book that blacks are being employed in large numbers for news jobs. The opposite is true. Long-standing prejudices and ignorance have kept blacks out of white journalism for years, and this condition still exists. Dr. Edward J. Trayes, associate professor of communications at Temple University, found in a recent survey that black participation on daily newspaper staffs was at an "extremely low level and quite disproportionate to the growing Negro population throughout America." His findings revealed that of the 7,152 news executives, editors, reporters and photographers on 196 daily newspapers of over 10,000 circulation, 111, or 1.55 per cent, were black. Only five executives were black. Of the 3,691 reporters represented in the study, eighty-three, or 2.25 per cent, were black. Professor Trayes concluded that out of the total number of news personnel, only about one in sixty-five was black. Of 775 photographers counted in the study, fifteen, or 1.9 per cent, were black. Worst of all, of the 196 newspapers surveyed, 149 reported having no black newsmen at all!

The ratio of blacks to whites in broadcast journalism is even smaller. At this writing, the three major television networks have only six black broadcasters among them and only a handful of blacks are reporting for local outlets. The picture is not noticeably brighter in magazines, although there are some outstanding departures from the rule. Ernest Dunbar, a black man, was a senior editor of *Look* magazine, and a smattering of blacks write for other news magazines. John Dotson, also black, is *Newsweek* magazine's bureau chief in Los Angeles. More about these men later.

Despite these figures, opportunities for blacks in journalism are increasing and will continue to rise in the next few years. The breakthrough has been made. Virtually all large daily newspapers have black reporters and photographers. What is even more encouraging is that editors are actively seeking black newsmen and women. In some instances this is tokenism, but not in most cases. The editors realize that black reporters are needed to cover the black communities.

Often they can gain access to news sources where white reporters cannot. For many years, news of blacks and their activities was reported only in the Negro press, with few exceptions. In recent years, newspapers have belatedly admitted that the black community has been woefully unrepresented in the news, although blacks are subscribers and buy the products advertised in the papers. The big-city dailies, particularly, have attempted to make up for the years of neglect by assigning reporters, both black and white, to ghetto areas. The *Washington Post* has seventeen black reporters, not a large number when one considers that Washington is predominantly black. The *San Francisco Examiner*, which did not employ one black reporter or cameraman from 1951 to 1961, now has its own training program for black newsmen, a sprinkling of whom are working for the city's news media. *The New York Times* has about fourteen black reporters and also has opened a Harlem bureau with Charlayne Hunter, a black woman, in charge. Miss Hunter, the first black to be admitted to the University of Georgia, is a highly talented writer whose work also has appeared in national magazines.

It's also an encouraging sign that more blacks are entering journalism schools, which are providing a pipeline to the news media for them. In addition, the Association for Education in Journalism is sponsoring special summer programs directed by Dr. Lionel Barrow, Jr. for young blacks interested in journalism careers. They are awarded internships with news organizations and also get special instruction at a university. The American Newspaper Publishers Association and other groups are furnishing scholarships to blacks majoring in journalism. The *St. Louis Post-Dispatch,* for example, furnishes $1,500 annual scholarships for black high school students planning to study journalism in college. Other black scholarships in journalism have been available at Columbia University in New York City.

The young black men and women getting jobs are covering not only the black community. Editors are discovering that they are capable of doing anything that white reporters can do. The black journalists are not being judged by their color but by what they can produce. Said one white editor: "When a black man or woman comes into this newsroom, they have to meet the same standards as anyone else. We may hire them because they are black, but once here they're on their own. They can be advanced in pay and status or be fired—like anyone else."

. Blacks who do make it are very much in evidence. Thomas A. Johnson, a black *New York Times* reporter, specializes in racial matters but quite frequently writes general news. He is considered one of the *Times'* top men. Richard Prince, a young *Washington Post* reporter, covers the city's district hall, handling all kinds of municipal items.

On the other hand, some black reporters prefer to cover the black community. Among them is L. F. "Lu" Palmer of the *Chicago Daily News*, a onetime staff member of the Chicago *Defender*, a black newspaper. Palmer covers black news four days a week and writes a syndicated column expressing a black point of view on Saturday. Ernest Johnston, Jr., of the *New York Post* also specializes in racial matters. A number of others will be discussed in this book.

Blacks who want to write exclusively about black affairs run into opposition from white editors who were weaned on the theory that a journeyman reporter should be able to cover any kind of story. Conversely, some black reporters resent being assigned only to ghetto stories. These are issues which have yet to be worked out on many newspapers. Harry M. Rosenfeld, *Washington Post* metropolitan editor, said he felt "uncomfortable" with the demand that only blacks cover the black community.

"I think I understand the reason for this insistence," Rosenfeld continued. "It's a means of encouraging the use of more blacks on daily newspapers, and I'm entirely in agreement with this desire. The big-city papers should be more representative of their communities. But I also believe that a newspaper should tell about the *whole* community. I would be unhappy if I could only assign a black to cover a black story just as I would be unhappy if I had to assign a Jew to a Jewish story or an Italian to an Italian story." A *Chicago Daily News* editor said that a similar policy is in force on that newspaper.

The New York Times, which at this moment has fourteen or more black reporters and photographers, sends them out on any kind of story but prefers to use them for racial matters when it appears necessary, according to editors. They say that no reporter is restricted in what he can cover and that it is not uncommon for white newsmen to cover race stories and for blacks to get general news assignments. Paul Delaney, for example, is a black reporter in the *Times'* Washington bureau, where he writes various kinds of government stories.

Being assigned to a "black beat" is not always an ideal situation for a black reporter. Some encounter hostility from community blacks, who have hurled such names at the newsmen as "Uncle Tom," "spy" and "sell-out."

The black journalist's problem of acceptance by black news sources was hurt by the government's attempt in 1970 to legally force Earl Caldwell, a black *New York Times* reporter, to surrender his notes and tape recordings of his interviews with Black Panther leaders. However, the United States Court of Appeals ruled recently that Caldwell did not have to reveal his record of the interviews. This was a victory not only for Caldwell and the *Times*, but for the entire news profession. Few things are more sacred to a reporter than his promise to protect his news suppliers. If these sources feel they cannot trust the newsman or that his word can be overturned by a government order, they will no longer give him information.

Other problems faced by today's black journalist include the matter of objectivity. American journalism in the last fifty years or so has developed a tradition of objectivity. This means that the reporter writes news stories without bias, giving both sides of controversial issues. The newsman's own thoughts and feelings are not supposed to enter the story. This is called straight reporting, with the emphasis on facts, not opinion. The latter belongs on the editorial page, according to the theory of objectivity.

The theory has been found unacceptable by a number of black journalists, who see it as an unworkable, if not insulting, idea. One of their conflicts arises from their efforts to be fair and objective while having little or no faith in the concept. This is an especially painful experience for those who formerly worked for black newspapers, most of which don't try to report such matters as civil rights in an objective way. Arguments between white editors and black reporters over objectivity have broken out in more than one newsroom.

Robert A. DeLeon, a black who worked for *The Atlanta Constitution* and *Newsday*, a big Long Island, New York, newspaper, recalled those days with a bitterness echoed by many of his black colleagues.

Once involved in the black community, I found it increasingly difficult to remain in the position of objective

observer and soon learned that such attempts were
futile. The first recognition of this futility came when
I realized that my biases and subjectivity entered into
the picture even before I began reporting a story. Because white papers and the media, in general, traditionally have neglected and, in fact, ignored the black
community, editors provided little guidance in the selection of stories in the black community. The whole
process of selection became a personal matter.

So, from the very beginning, I had to dismiss the
notion of objectivity. In choosing stories I constantly
found that I was seeking good things that were being
done in the black community. The attempts were to
accentuate the positive rather than the negative in an
unconscious effort, I guess, to prove to whites that
blacks were human and wanted, basically, to share in
the same things as everyone else. For this bias I have
never apologized, because white journalists have been
doing it all along as it relates to the day-to-day happen-
ings in the white community.

Betty Washington, a black *Chicago Daily News* reporter,
said she strives for fairness in any story she covers "even
when I'm emotionally upset about something like a police-
Panther shoot-out. But my story is bound to be biased to a
certain extent. I don't care, because I know how other stories
are written in the paper. Actually, I don't believe that anyone is completely objective."

Her colleague, L. F. Palmer, agreed, terming objectivity
a "myth." He stated: "I believe in advocacy journalism, particularly for blacks. At the same time, I also feel that a reader
is in a better position to evaluate a story if the biases of the
writer are not hidden. It's when they're concealed that the

reader gets taken. If a reader knows that I am a pro-black writer, which I am, he can more competently deal with what I'm saying."

Another former *Newsday* reporter, Pat Patterson, who now edits a new magazine, *Black Enterprise*, said: "To report on events that affect the black community, with its laundry list of ills and depressing conditions, makes it difficult to reject the role of advocate and maintain a sense of balance needed to report an unbiased story."

Grievances of black newsmen have led them into forming their own organizations as a means of expression. One is a nationwide group called the National Conference of Black News Media Workers. Rush Greenlee, a black San Francisco journalist, said the conference was formed because "there is a hunger among black newsmen to know who they are, to clarify the role they have been playing and the one they might play in the black liberation struggle." Local units of black newsmen also have been established in New York, Philadelphia, Chicago and San Francisco.

There is evidence that newspapers are becoming increasingly aware of dissatisfaction among some black editorial workers and are trying to eliminate the causes. Some black newsmen are being trained as specialists in black affairs. Older black reporters and editors are available on various newspapers to discuss grievances with younger black staff members. The Fort Worth *Star-Telegram* lets black reporters take their turn on assignments just as any other reporter. Editor Jack Butler said: "We send our black newsmen to all sorts of public functions. My instructions to the city desk are that if one of these reporters is not welcome at such a function, we will consider that the *Star-Telegram* is not welcome." The editor of another metropolitan paper declared: "Some of our black reporters felt that they should be

assigned only to black stories. They couldn't be for a variety
of reasons, one of them being that they were not ready to
handle certain complex stories. Also, other reporters were
interested in the same stories, and the problems of scheduling
made it impossible. This was explained to the black reporters
and generally accepted."

The opportunities for blacks in broadcast journalism also
are expanding, but there are some differences in comparison
to newspapers. Because television is primarily an entertainment medium, the people selected—black and white—for on-
the-air positions are those who are photogenic, have good
voices and are rich in poise and personality. One could be a
first-rate journalist and yet not qualify to announce the news
for a TV network or station.

Off-camera jobs, however, are usually not dependent on
the applicant's looks or voice. These include news writing,
shooting pictures, film editing and, for the more experienced
person, assignment editor and producer. Journalism schools
provide training for these duties as well as for announcing.
The ideal candidate for a broadcasting job is one who has a
firm grasp of the basic journalistic skills—reporting and
writing—and on-the-air qualities. It's usually best to start a
broadcasting career on a small or medium-size station, but
the major networks and metropolitan area stations have
hired black men and women with little or no experience.
Among the blacks now in television journalism are such
well-known persons as Bob Teague, William Matney, Gil
Noble, Melba Tolliver, Art Rust, Jr., Lucille Rich and Hal
Walker.

Radio is a medium that has provided more journalism
jobs than television. Almost every town in America—big or
small—has at least one radio station, and all broadcast news.
In many cases, though, it is a "rip and read" operation, mean-

ing that news is taken off the Associated Press or United Press International teletypes and read over the air. AP and UPI are two of the world's largest press associations, having bureaus all over the globe. The two wire services sell their services to newspapers, broadcasters, magazines and other news outlets.

A smooth voice is a help for radio newscasting, but again there are writing spots that require no on-the-air reading. The important element for both radio and television is a sound understanding of what news is, how to get it and how to write it. Journalism is a business that calls for speed, accuracy and enterprise. Whether one is reporting for the print or the broadcast media, he must learn journalistic principles and use them. Errors can bring libel suits and may damage the reporter's reputation and that of his paper or station. Also, writing, be it for the printed page or the microphone, must be clear and compelling. It must arouse interest.

Magazine jobs also are opening up for blacks, but not as rapidly as in newspapers and broadcasting. Most blacks in this area work for the growing number of black magazines. These include the renowned *Ebony, Essence* (for women), *Black Enterprise, Jet, Tan, Elegant, Negro Traveler, Black World* and others. Blacks are breaking into white magazines, and more are being sought. Both *Time* and *Newsweek* have black reporters. Gordon Parks writes and photographs for *Life.* Charlayne Hunter was a staff writer for the *New Yorker* before going to *The New York Times.* The number is not large, but the trend has started and is not likely to stop.

The door also has been opened in public relations and in advertising. These jobs are mostly available in New York, Chicago, Los Angeles and other large media centers.

A solid background in newspaper or wire-service reporting

is a valuable aid for getting jobs in public relations. The
P.R. man represents a client whose name he must get before
the public through newspapers and other media. He must
be able to communicate skillfully and come up with ideas
that editors will want to print or broadcast. The young man
or woman who has worked for publications knows what
editors seek and the format in which they accept materials.

Both public relations and advertising training can be obtained from schools and departments of journalism. The
main difference between P.R. and advertising is that the
latter appears in printed space or on air time which is purchased. The P.R. expert aims at getting his message into
the media free.

Both advertising and public relations take in a variety of
tasks. The advertising man may be an artist, copywriter,
idea man or account executive. Public relations calls for such
skills as writing, creating ideas and consulting with clients.
In addition to the public-relations agencies which represent
clients on a fee basis, there are dozens of other kinds of
P.R. jobs. Virtually every major organization has a public-
relations director and/or staff. Among them are General
Motors, the American Cancer Society, the National Association for the Advancement of Colored People, universities,
hospitals, trade unions, charitable groups and many others.
One of the biggest public-relations employers is the United
States government. Almost every one of its departments
and branches has a P.R. apparatus. These fields will be de-
tailed in a later chapter.

2 / The Black Press— Yesterday and Today

Should a black man or woman interested in journalism seek a job on an established white news medium, or should he contribute his talents to the black press? Thomas A. Johnson, who is black and a leading *New York Times* reporter, says that this decision is up to each individual but adds:

"If the student absorbs the skills and gets as much exposure as he can to the American realities, he will be in a better position to decide on his future in journalism."

Those who opt for black publications will carry on a tradition that began on March 16, 1827, when two men who believed the time had come for a means of black expression founded *Freedom's Journal* in New York City. The editors were John Russwurm, the first black to graduate from an American college (Bowdoin), and Samuel E. Cornish, a minister and writer. Russwurm, for whom a newspaper writing award has been named, later resigned from the *Journal* and sailed for Africa, where he became the editor of the *Liberia Herald*, a pioneer African newspaper. In the *Journal's* first issue, Cornish and Russwurm wrote:

"It is our earnest wish to make our *Journal* a medium of intercourse between our brethren in the different states of this great confederacy; that through its columns an expression of our sentiments on many interesting subjects which concern us may be offered to the public: that plans which apparently are beneficial may be candidly discussed and properly weighed."

The *Journal's* editorial policy was built on the following themes: black assertion, the black image, education for blacks, economic improvement, civil rights and African renaissance. The little four-page weekly was calling for the abolition of slavery four years before a white editor, William Lloyd Garrison, began printing his famous abolitionist newspaper, the *Liberator*. The editors of *Freedom's Journal* frankly admitted that it was a propaganda organ, declaring that such a publication was necessary to fight a "backward institution."

The *Journal* eventually disappeared, but its cause was taken up twenty years later by Frederick Douglass, the son of a slave mother, who escaped from the South and founded an antislavery newspaper, the *North Star*, in Rochester, New York. Douglass, also a noted lecturer and orator, at first followed Garrison's line, but later advocated a more conservative approach to ending slavery. After the Civil War, Douglass became marshal of the District of Columbia and later American minister to Haiti.

By the end of the Civil War, there were about thirty black newspapers. It was thought that the defeat of the South and the freeing of the slaves would eliminate the need for a black press, but the assassination of President Abraham Lincoln dispelled this idea. The black press continued to publish in the face of mounting prejudice against blacks. By 1880 there were still twenty-one black journals in New York, Washington, Norfolk, Cleveland, Philadelphia and other cities, most of them one-man operations and printed for the most part in plants owned by whites. A major handicap for the black publishers was that there were so few blacks skilled at reporting and printing. The printing crafts for years refused apprenticeships to blacks, a fact that is not noticeably changed today.

At the beginning of the First World War, there were more than two hundred black newspapers scattered around the nation. Many of these publications were more radical than their forerunners, adopting such names as *Challenge, Crusader, Emancipator* and *Messenger*. Indeed, some of them were too militant for the United States Department of Justice, which took action to suppress them. One of the most influential black papers was the *New York Age*. It was inclined to be conservative, arguing that change was necessary but that it should come through orderly democratic processes. Other black newspapers and magazines were urging change through revolutionary action.

Although the *Age* stopped well short of pushing for violent overthrow of the government, it nevertheless fought hard for reforms, including the abolition of separate schools, a civil-rights bill and the right of blacks to serve in the Spanish-American War. The *Age's* editor was T. Thomas Fortune, a brilliant writer who had once been an assistant to the editor of the New York *Evening Sun*, a white newspaper. In his book *Inside Black America*, Roi Ottley asserted that Fortune was the most widely read black editor of his time and that his editorials were often the subject of comment by white dailies. When Theodore Roosevelt was police commissioner of New York, he was reputed to have said to Fortune: "Tom, for God's sake keep that pen of yours off me." After Roosevelt became President of the United States, he summoned Fortune to the White House for an important assignment. The black journalist was sent to the Hawaiian and Philippine islands to investigate complaints by the islanders and general conditions there.

In 1909, when the *Age* was still riding high, it got its first serious competition. With his only equipment consisting of six sheets of paper and a pencil, James H. Anderson established the *Amsterdam News* in Harlem, taking the name from the street where he lived. The *Age* is long dead, but the *Amsterdam News* remains as one of the most important black weeklies in the United States. When it was sold in 1971 to an all-black group headed by Manhattan Borough President Percy E. Sutton and Clarence B. Jones, lawyer and stockbroker, it had a circulation of more than 82,600 in the New York metropolitan area. This was thought to be the largest circulation for any black community-based paper in the country.

At about the same time the *Amsterdam News* was born in New York, the Midwest produced a black newspaper that was to become equally formidable. It was called the *Chicago Defender*, and its publisher was Robert Abbott, who started it as a flimsy handbill. In 1910 the *Defender* began attracting readers with sensational headlines and stories. Instead of playing up to the black intellectual as many black journals were doing, the *Defender* aimed its appeal at the mass of blacks who had migrated from the South. By 1922 the *Defender's* circulation was over 100,000. It gained popularity by ballyhooing the North as the "Promised Land" in which oppressed blacks from the South could find a home, opportunities for employment and education for their children. The *Defender* also crusaded against discrimination in the South.

But the paper fell on hard times during the Great Depression of the 1930s. Abbott stepped down and turned over the reins to John H. Sengstacke, who had started as a bookkeeper in the organization. At that point the *Defender* was nearly bankrupt and Sengstacke didn't even have money to meet the payroll. He applied for a loan to nearly every Chicago bank and was refused each time. "They weren't lending money to Negro businesses," Sengstacke recalled.

The new publisher finally got a loan from a small South Side bank, and he was on his way. The paper went daily in 1956. Sengstacke estimates that today the *Defender* runs 90 per cent black news and 10 per cent general news.

A lively competitor of the *Defender* was the *Chicago Whip*, which originated the boycott strategy in the 1920s as a means of getting blacks jobs in the city's largely black South Side. The newspaper bannered the slogan: "Don't Spend Your Money Where You Can't Work." The campaign was the forerunner of a number of successful black campaigns against discrimination in hiring.

Another influential black newspaper, the *Pittsburgh Courier*, began publication in 1910. A few weeks later it was taken over by Robert Lee Vann, a lawyer, who made it a powerful organ that was to command a circulation of more than 250,000 by World War II. Vann himself also gained prominence as a politician and was a special assistant in the Attorney General's office during the administration of President Franklin D. Roosevelt.

World War II gave the black press an excellent opportunity to blast discrimination in the armed forces, and most papers took full advantage of it. Their campaigns were so effective that President Harry Truman declared an end to Jim Crow in the services. During this time black weeklies also waged a successful fight for fair employment practices.

Some black newspapers covered the war itself. The *Defender* had five correspondents in the field while the *Afro-American* had eight, including the first black woman war correspondent, Elizabeth M. Phillips. The *Pittsburgh Courier* hired Walter Merguson, a onetime Chicago postal clerk and a World War I veteran, as its man in France. Merguson had stayed in France after World War I, becoming a tourist guide. He used to drive black travelers out to the old battlefields in a beat-up jalopy, and then send items about the excursions to the *Courier*. Editor Vann was so impressed that he gave Merguson a full-time job as the paper's European correspondent. Shortly after World War II broke out, Merguson scored a beat on the entire American press corps by filing a story on the French mobilization of a black army composed of 2,000,000 colonial soldiers and 500,000 laborers. *The New York Times* later confirmed the report from Paris.

The black press enjoyed a rapid growth between the First and Second World Wars, mainly because of the continued trek of blacks to the cities and their increasing literacy. In 1943 there were 164 black newspapers, fifty-eight of which were published in twenty cities of 50,000 or more black residents. Most of the papers were weeklies, and two-thirds of them were in the South. The most important newspapers, however, were and are still published in the North. Two others which gained prominence during this period were the Baltimore *Afro-American* and the Norfolk (Virginia) *Journal and Guide*. The *Chicago Defender* became a daily in 1956 and began publishing a special national edition that was sold around the country. The *Courier* and the *Afro-American* became national weeklies after World War II. Among the *Afro-American* contributors was Langston Hughes, the black poet.

Today the picture has changed in various ways. The *Defender*, the *Afro-American* and the *Amsterdam News* are still important black journals with healthy circulations, but they face strong competition. *Muhammad Speaks* leads the field with an estimated circulation above 400,000. Another newcomer, *Black Panther*, boasts 110,000, mostly in street sales. The *Michigan Chronicle* and the Los Angeles *Sentinel* also are coming along rapidly. Some of the old leaders, such as the *Courier* and the *Journal and Guide*, have lost circulation. The decline is laid partly to television, which also has cut into the circulation of white dailies. People are finding it easier to get their news through the tube or on the radio. There's not as much of it, but it is digested more easily. The editor of a black paper in Chicago said that the four black-oriented radio stations in the community reach more black listeners in an hour than his paper can in a month.

One element remains the same today. The black newspapers still exist largely on the presentation of black news—news that the white papers usually ignore. This is the principal reason the black press emerged in the first place. The births, deaths, marriages, successes and problems of blacks dominate the pages of the black community newspapers. When news of the larger world is reported, it is often slanted for black appeal to give the item more meaning for the reader. The ultramilitant papers, such as *Black Panther*, put little stress on community activities, reserving most of their news space for stories about oppression and injustice. These stories, along with those of crime and riots, also are displayed on the front pages of such old-line newspapers as the Chicago *Daily Defender* and the *Amsterdam News*.

L. F. Palmer, Jr., wrote in the spring, 1970, issue of the *Columbia Journalism Review*:

"Today, with the black revolution at its zenith, the question is raised throughout the ghettos: where is the black press? The answer is that the established black press is squarely in the middle of a dilemma. It finds itself trying not to be too conservative for the black revolutionaries, and not too revolutionary for white conservatives upon whom it depends for advertising. . . . Some reporters on black newspapers, moreover, do not appear to have the dedication to the black cause which characterized black newsmen a couple of decades ago. . . ."

Black newspapers also have the problem of getting and keeping reporters, editors and advertising personnel. Not enough black newsmen are being produced to feed both the black and the white newspapers. In most cases the latter are paying more money, and black editors find themselves in the frustrating position of training young men and women who are lured away by the white dailies. This has happened in New York, Chicago, Detroit and Los Angeles. White newspapers and magazines also are watching the journalism schools for black graduates. One such young man at New York University had offers from four Establishment dailies, each trying to outbid the other. He finally went to a metropolitan newspaper which paid him the highest starting salary it had ever given a cub reporter. "Please don't tell anyone how much you're getting," an editor asked him.

Today there are between 250 and 300 black newspapers with a circulation of more than two million. Some are prospering, while others are fighting to stay alive in the face of soaring costs and competition from other media. A number of black papers are published for a few months and then disappear. Besides those already named, some of the most prominent black newspapers are the St. Louis *Mirror*, the Los Angeles *Herald-Dispatch*, the San Francisco *Sun-Reporter*, the Cleveland *Call & Post*, the Atlanta *Daily World*, the Washington, D.C., *Informer*, the Indianapolis *Herald*, the Chicago *Courier*, the *Atlanta World*, the New York *Courier*, the Memphis *Tri-State Defender*, the Kansas City (Missouri) *Call* and the *Louisiana Weekly* in New Orleans.

Some of these weeklies exert strong influence in the black community. Carl E. Stokes, Cleveland's former black mayor, credited the Cleveland *Call & Post* as "the most fundamental factor in the development of my career as a young politician. It meant that my story would be told week after week."

William H. Lee, publisher of the Sacramento (California) *Observer* and secretary of the National Newspaper Publishers Association, a black group, said in a *New York Times* interview that the association is "attempting to deal with the wide-ranging, substantive issues that affect black people." Frank L. Stanley, publisher of the Louisville *Defender*, asserted that black newspapers experienced a 33.3 per cent growth from 1961 to 1971.

It's clear that these weeklies serve Negro interests in a way that white dailies do not, despite the latter's efforts in the past decade to give more and better coverage of the black community. The riots of the 1960s in Watts, California, Newark, New Jersey, Chicago and other cities finally drove home to some white papers the urgent need for a wider understanding of the black man in the ghetto and his miseries. The point was underscored by the presidentially appointed Kerner Commission, which, after the riots, recommended that daily newspapers find, motivate and hire representative numbers of blacks and other minority-group members.

The dailies have learned some lessons, but there is still plenty of evidence that the message has not got all the way through. Lawrence Schneider, professor of journalism at the University of Washington, reported that his community relations study revealed a serious cultural gap separating blacks and white middle-class reporters. According to the survey, reporters do not write stories from direct observation of the black community and they do not seek "firsthand interviews" with blacks.

"In many cases not only is there no sympathy for the minorities but prejudice prevails," Professor Schneider said.

Another journalism professor, Guido H. Stempel III of

Ohio University, discovered the same lack of recognition of blacks in his study entitled "Visibility of Blacks in News Magazines and News Picture Magazines, 1960 and 1970." Stempel found that the "visibility" of blacks in these publications had increased in ten years, but he asked: "Is this enough visibility?" The educator added that "what a reader sees is largely a reflection of a segregated society."

Such surveys emphasize that the black press plays the vital role of hammering home the issues of equal representation in American society. "The Negro press is essentially and inescapably a protest press," wrote Henry Lee Moon, press secretary of the National Association for the Advancement of Colored People in *Race and the News Media*. "It is an integral part of the civil rights movement, not only the recorder but also the voice of Negro protest. The press knows that the so-called revolution did not begin May 17, 1954, with the U.S. Supreme Court school desegregation decision, or on February 1, 1960, with the student sit-in in Greensboro, North Carolina. It knows that there has never been a time in the history of the nation when some segment of the Negro population was not in revolt against the inferior status imposed upon the race. At no time has the entire race been directly involved in the struggle, but at all times since the founding of the republic, the shadow of the race issue has hovered grimly over our national life."

BLACK MAGAZINES

Black magazines are not blooming as profusely as black newspapers in America, but they are becoming available in greater numbers. And, like the newspapers, they have a history deeply rooted in the black struggle.

The first black magazine in the United States is believed

to have been *Mirror of Liberty*, published in 1838 by David Ruggles, an abolitionist who voiced the dreams and aspirations of black Americans. *Southern Workman*, published in Hampton, Virginia, about 1872, and *A.M.E. Church Review*, begun in Philadelphia in 1844, were concerned mainly with religious, educational and literary affairs.

The first really influential black periodical was *Crisis*, edited by the noted scholar and author W. E. B. Du Bois after the turn of the century. A native of Great Barrington, Massachusetts, Du Bois was of Negro, French and Dutch descent. He was a graduate of Fisk and Harvard universities and later studied at the University of Berlin. A proud, aloof man who usually wore a high hat, cane and white gloves, Du Bois was in the group of black intellectuals who swung away from the conciliatory attitude of the black scientist Booker T. Washington.

After teaching at various universities, Du Bois took the helm of *Crisis* in 1910 and made it a potent organ for protest. In his own column, "As the Crow Flies," he was by turns sarcastic, witty, urbane and angry. The magazine featured drawings by black artists and ran stories of black achievements. *Crisis*, a New York publication, was nominally the "house" magazine for the NAACP, but Du Bois, a crusty loner, pretty much ran it his own way. He struck out against wrongs inflicted on blacks, called for the liberation of African colonies and carried on feuds with blacks whose programs he disliked. He launched one of his bitterest attacks against Marcus Garvey, the leader of the "Back to Africa" movement, which he publicized in his weekly newspaper, *Negro World*.

Du Bois also created a quarterly magazine, *Phylon: The Atlanta University Review of Race and Culture*, when he taught sociology at that institution in 1940. *Phylon*, the Greek word for race, was a successful experiment in publishing a magazine that introduced into the social sciences the life and culture of black people. It was, and is, a scholarly journal for students of history, education and sociology.

Du Bois joined the Communist Party in 1961 at the age of ninety-three. He died two years later in Ghana, shortly after becoming a citizen of that country.

Another black magazine in the early years of the twentieth century was *Opportunity*, an organ of the Urban League. Both *Crisis* and *Opportunity* published stories, poems and essays by black writers.

In 1917 a black periodical appeared that soon outstripped both *Crisis* and *Opportunity* in readership. It began as the *Hotel Messenger*, a voice for the Headwaiters and Sidewaiters Society of Greater New York. But when the magazine took a radical turn and also attacked the "grafting" of headwaiters by shaking down waiters, the headwaiters withdrew their support. The magazine then became simply the *Messenger*, acquiring at the same time two new editors, A. Philip Randolph and Chandler Owen, both lecturers at the Rand School of Social Science. Randolph was later to become organizer and president of the Brotherhood of Sleeping Car Porters.

The editors lost no time in letting readers know where they stood: well to the left of center. The publication's prospectus proclaimed it as "the only magazine of scientific radicalism in the world published by Negroes." The editors promised "to lift our pens above the cringing demagogy of the times and above the cheap peanut politics of the old, reactionary, Negro leaders." This was mild stuff compared to the content of today's radical black media, but at that time it was enough to start the Establishment quivering. A state legislative committee assailed the *Messenger* as "by far the most dangerous of all Negro publications." White and black conservatives had even more to think about when the *Messenger* in 1918 was credited with convincing 25 per cent of New York's blacks to vote for the Socialist Party's black candidate for Congress. The *Messenger* folded in 1929.

Nothing much happened to black magazines until World War II, when a number of new ones appeared on the newsstands. Many were picture magazines on the order of *Life* and *Look* and were aimed primarily at a middle-class audience. The most prominent of these publications were *Ebony*, *Jet*, *Hue* and *Tan Confessions*, which later became *Tan*. *Ebony*, the leading black magazine today, dealt with the achievements of blacks while giving readers a glimpse into their personal lives. Other magazines featured romantic or sensational stories very much like those in certain white publications. E. Franklin Frazier, the black historian, wrote in 1957:

"Although the Negro press, including magazines as well as newspapers, claims to be published in the interest of the 'race,' it represents primarily the interests of the black bourgeoisie and promulgates the bourgeois values of the make-believe world of the black bourgeoisie."

Ebony has never pretended to be a spokesman for radical blacks, but in recent years it has published a number of articles which highlight the race crisis in America.

Many of the World War II publications died in postwar years, but *Ebony* and several others are alive and well. In fact, the trend is toward more black magazines to match the rising literacy among blacks and the expanding Negro market for advertisers' goods and services. Most magazines depend on advertising for their existence, and the black periodicals are no exception.

Ebony is among several black magazines published in the

1970s. In addition to those named in the first chapter, the magazines include *Freedomways, Interracial Review, Tuesday* (a newspaper supplement), the *Journal of Negro History, Southern School News, Liberation, Amistad, Teen Elegant* and *Black Scholar.* The last is a serious publication that analyzes the black experience in America from a black point of view. First published in 1969, the magazine has offered articles by such writers as Sékou Touré, Stokely Carmichael, Eldridge Cleaver, Amiri Baraka (Leroi Jones) and John O. Killens. *Black Scholar* also has given space to young black authors, including Joyce Ladner and James Turner. The periodical is directed toward students, professors and other black intellectuals.

But the biggest name in black magazines is the Johnson Publishing Company, whose varied activities are conducted from a modest two-story building on South Michigan Avenue in Chicago. The firm, which produces *Ebony, Tan, Black World* and *Jet,* is headed by John H. Johnson, a fifty-one-year-old tycoon who grew up in rural Arkansas and spent most of his youth in Chicago's South Side ghetto. *Ebony's* circulation has gone over the million mark, and its revenue is about seven million dollars a year. A slick color job, *Ebony* generally reflects the tastes and attitude of the more affluent blacks—a policy that is not universally welcomed in the black community. In recent years, however, *Ebony* has interlaced its articles about the "good life" with searing pieces about the black protest movement. It was one of the first national publications to air Stokely Carmichael's views, and its senior editor, Lerone Bennett, Jr., was the first to use the term "Black Power." Johnson explained: "We were moderate when the Negro population was moderate, and we became militant when our readers became more militant."

Ebony has featured articles with such titles as "Black Politics in the New South," "Dilemma of the Black Policeman," "Black Hospital Struggles to Survive" and "The World of the Slave," a historical look at the effects of slavery in the United States. The author, Lerone Bennett, wrote:

> . . . The mark of the slave, the mark of the *creative* slave is deep in the flesh of every American. . . . America is in large part what it is because of what it tried to do to the slave. . . . As a matter of fact one can say . . . that slavery is the key to the meaning of America.
>
> It was slavery and the slave trade which provided the initial thrust to the American economy. It was slavery which built Monticello, Mount Vernon and Boston and Charleston and New Orleans. Slavery shaped the white founding fathers. It shaped and molded the fundamental compromises of the U.S. Constitution. It shaped and molded the Westward movement and the Civil War. . . .

Ebony's mixture of politics, sports, entertainment and personalities also published articles headed "The Quiet Life of Muhammad Ali," "Best-Dressed Black Women," "Ike and Tina Turner," "Judy Pace—The Thinking Man's Star," "World's Leading Heart Transplant Sets Super Pace" and "100 Most Influential Black Americans." The latter list includes two working journalists, columnist Carl Rowan and Lerone Bennett, and two publishers, John H. Johnson and John H. Sengstacke, publisher of the Chicago *Daily Defender* and other newspapers.

To critics who fault *Ebony* for not being militant enough, Managing Editor Hans J. Massaquoi gives this reply:

"*Ebony* is first of all a moneymaking venture. It's a business just as are many other magazines. We can only do the things to advance the black cause if we are solvent. *Ebony* is edited to appeal to as broad an audience as possible. So we have a variety of articles. We feel we have material in the magazine that appeals to young people, old people, intellectuals and perhaps to illiterates. I think our steadily rising circulation is an indication that we've come up with a successful formula."

Few would disagree with the last statement. In a period when many magazines, black and white, were dropping by the wayside, *Ebony*, a well-edited and well-written publication, managed to surge ahead to a point where it is almost as well known in the white world as in the black. A number of big-time advertisers consider it a good medium for their products, and it continues to make money. After *Ebony* was launched in 1945, it took John Johnson almost a year to land any advertising. The publisher began a letter-writing campaign to the heads of large corporations, asserting that "if the president of the world's smallest country came to the United States, he would be met by the American president as a matter of protocol." As the president of a small, struggling concern, Johnson claimed the right to be received by the heads of the corporations. The gimmick got Johnson an appointment with the president of the Zenith Radio Corporation, who gave the publisher his first big advertising account. Zenith has been an *Ebony* advertiser ever since. *Ebony's* success inspired Johnson to create two other money-makers, *Jet* and *Tan*, in 1950 and 1951 respectively.

Ebony recruits its staff members from different sources. In some cases a writer may have made a name for himself on another publication and attracts *Ebony's* interest. Some young editorial employees simply wrote and asked for a job. Others were hired off newspapers, both white and black. At the moment, the staff is black, mostly young and college-educated. Said Massaquoi: "We don't insist on a college degree, but we do like our writers to demonstrate talent and a certain sensitivity to what is going on in the black community." Massaquoi said *Ebony* pays starting salaries to editorial workers which are comparable with those paid on the general magazines. He continued: "I deplore the attitude of some black journalists who feel that, because they are working for the general press, they are connected with some kind of superior medium. This notion sprung from the time when the black weekly was perhaps not a model of typography, grammar or syntax. But all that is changed now. There are now some excellent black newspapers and magazines. I don't think that any black journalist will be stepping down if he writes for black publications."

Hans Massaquoi was born and raised in Germany, the son of a German mother and African father. He came to the United States in 1950, and after army service studied journalism at the University of Illinois. He later did graduate work at Northwestern University. When he was ready to start his career, he pounded on the doors of white daily and weekly newspapers in vain. He eventually was hired by the Johnson Publishing Company as a reporter on *Jet* magazine.

Ebony's sister magazine, *Black World*, with a circulation of about 70,000, takes a more passionate view of the black revolt. The publication urges its readers to toss aside white attitudes in favor of strictly black attitudes in education, culture and politics. Its editor, Hoyt Fuller, a graduate of Wayne State University, said in an interview with *Time* magazine: "I don't expect things to change from the white side, so I'm working to change things from the black side." He also criticized middle-class blacks, observing that "my experience with [them] has been that all their efforts have been directed toward identifying with whites, emulating white people. They are not helping the black community to survive."

In recent months, *Black World* has presented a combination of black-slanted articles, short stories, poetry and literary criticism. Among the articles have been "The News Media: Racism's First Line of Defense," "The Challenge of Blackness," "The Emergence of Black National Consciousness in America" and "The Meaning of Black History."

Freedomways, a serious quarterly, also serves up heavy reading in such articles as "The GI Movement vs. the War," "Art and Liberation" and "Paul Robeson: Black Warrior." In addition, there are stories, poems and book reviews.

A comparative newcomer on the scene, *Black Enterprise*, is a lively, slick-paper monthly that spotlights the swelling number of blacks entering the business world in roles traditionally held by whites. The article titles tell the story: "Black Auto Dealers," "Western Electric Plugs in Black Suppliers" and "Black Image Makers on Madison Avenue," about black advertising agencies and executives. *Black Enterprise* also examines the economic climate with such pieces as "The Returning GI: What Does He Do Now?" and "What to Do About Crime," a report on what crime is costing the black community.

The magazine's editor is Pat Patterson, a former newspaperman for both black and white papers, who said in an editorial that ". . . for the first time in our history in this country we seem to be moving toward developing a black business community nationally."

A magazine for black women, *Essence*, was started in 1968 by four young black businessmen who raised a million dollars by convincing investors that there would be a strong market for a publication aimed at black college-educated or successful career women between the ages of eighteen and thirty-four. Two years later the magazine had a circulation of 150,-000 in 145 cities. The adventurous four were Jonathan Blount, Edward Lewis, Cecil Hollingsworth and Clarence Smith, who was the oldest at thirty-six.

Indications are that more black magazines will appear in the United States. Some of the current ones may die out, since publishing always has been a hazardous business. But it seems clear that this medium is important for black expression. Magazines can communicate in ways that television and newspapers can't, or at least not as effectively. At this moment two or three young black people may be planning a new magazine that will outsell *Ebony*. Such a venture takes money, imagination, talent and a belief in oneself. Today's black publishers and editors have shown that all these are possible.

3 / Black Newspapermen

Reporting is a tough business. It's even tougher for a black reporter. Usually he has a hard time getting a job, and things don't become much easier after that. In his own office he may be mistaken for a janitor or messenger. Some news sources refuse to talk to him, or are patronizing when they do. In certain situations he may be the only newsman asked to show his press card.

But there is one fact the black newsman knows. The door is open. Even though less than 5 per cent of the nation's reporters are black, a clear trend toward hiring blacks on daily newspapers is visible. Moreover, a growing number of black journalists are proving themselves the equal of whites. If these blacks were hired as a token gesture, their bosses have long ceased to think of them as symbols. Let's take a look at some of them.

THOMAS A. JOHNSON

Thomas A. Johnson is considered one of *The New York Times's* best reporters. As a specialist concentrating on the racial and social revolution in this country, he has won a number of awards, medals and citations for excellence in interpreting, analyzing and writing the news. A calm, heavyset man with a rich, baritone voice, Tom Johnson has reported from Vietnam, Europe, the Far East, South America and the West Indies, and has had many assignments in this country.

Johnson was born in St. Augustine, Florida, in 1928. He was graduated in journalism from Long Island University in 1954, earning his way in jobs ranging from clerk to construction worker. After college, he went into the United States Army for four years, becoming a sergeant major for an infantry battalion.

When he left the service Johnson wanted to be a reporter, but it was almost impossible for a black to find work of this kind on the white dailies. So he became a caseworker in the New York City Department of Welfare, counseling juvenile delinquents and their parents. On the surface this was far removed from journalism, but the experience in interviewing and investigation was to be extremely valuable to him in his later career as a newspaperman. "This was the best kind of training I could get," he recalled.

In 1960 Johnson's yearning for a journalism career took a more concrete form. He became owner and operator of a New York public-relations firm that served out-of-town newspapers and magazines.

By 1963 Johnson's business was doing very well, and he began to think less frequently about becoming a newspaperman. But one day he got a phone call from a friend, the late Louis Lomax, well-known black author and journalist. Lomax had been lecturing on Long Island, where he had heard that *Newsday*, the prosperous suburban daily, was seeking a black reporter, its first. Johnson inquired about the opening and was hired after an interview. On *Newsday*, he covered both racial and general assignment stories, developing his skills while acquiring a deeper understanding of the black revolution.

Three years later the revolution had gained momentum, and several dailies were looking for their first black reporter or were ready to add to those they already had. Among the

latter was *The New York Times*, the most influential paper
in the United States and a career goal for thousands of journalists. The *Times*, which selects its reporters in the manner
of a jeweler choosing between rare gems, heard of Johnson's
fine record at *Newsday* and approached him on the possi-
bility of his joining its staff. Most newsmen are so overawed
by a *Times* invitation that they would not think of saying
anything that might jeopardize their chances of being hired.
But Tom Johnson is not most newspapermen. His initial interview with a *Times* editor appeared to be going well when
he volunteered an opinion that the *Times* could be doing a
better job of reporting the black revolution. The editor was
taken aback, to say the least. For a relatively obscure journalist to question the *Times* reportage was virtually unheard
of—especially if he was interested in joining that august institution.

They argued about Johnson's views, and the editor began
liking what he heard. Here was a reporter with ideas! There
were three or four more interviews, and Tom Johnson was
offered a job, which he accepted. Since that time he has become one of the *Times*'s top-ranked reporters and the winner
of several journalistic awards, including the Urban League's
John Russwurm $1,000 prize for "sustained excellence in in-
terpreting, reporting and analyzing the news." He also has
earned the Metropolitan Newspaper Award for his article,
"Life on Welfare, A Daily Struggle for Existence." A series
on the United States Negro in Vietnam gained for Johnson
the Dumont Award for excellence in international journalism and the Page One Award for Foreign Reporting by the
Newspaper Guild of New York. Johnson has lectured in many
cities on his experiences and is an adjunct associate professor
of journalism at New York University. In 1968 he wrote a
documentary, "The Black Soldier," for CBS Television.

Johnson views his role and that of other black reporters very clearly. "Some years ago," he said, "blacks saw themselves as newsmen first, black second. Today, black reporters see themselves as interpreters of the black revolution. We are experts with a built-in file cabinet."

The "file cabinet," he explained, is the sum of the black man's experiences in the United States. Johnson scoffed at the idea held by some editors that covering black news requires no special education or preparation.

"This is not true," he asserted. "The black reporter by virtue of his color has an advantage over a white reporter in covering black news, but he needs training to be able to interpret and express what he knows instinctively through his experiences."

Johnson urged black youth interested in journalism to get high school and college training to give them the needed writing and other journalistic skills for their careers. He says:

I also would advise every new, young black journalist to develop the healthiest ego possible. Learn all you can about yourself—your strengths, your weaknesses—the things for which you are willing to die and the lies you can live with.

For the craft of journalism—there are some who make it simply a job and others who make it an art—will require that you take the world apart, chew it up, digest it and then tell humanity, in 500 words, what it all means.

Despite the awesome responsibility this implies, the job is and always has been done by a good many people who are uncaring and unfeeling and who simply apply the long-accepted tools of the craft—who, what, when, where and how—to whatever the job to be done. Like photographers, they all used the same basic instrument or set of tools for the job.

But the difference between any photographer and an Henri Cartier-Bresson or a Gordon Parks is that extra bit of himself, that spirit, spirituality, that "inner eye" or "soul" that these men bring to their tasks. Similar attitudes and commitments can be observed in the journalist who makes newspapering more meaningful to his time than just a column of type to fill a column of space.

Journalism tools, of course, are vital, and one does not move ahead without them. But they are easy to obtain and master. Much more difficult is the taking of that next step: developing the commitment to one's craft or art and knowing, as best as one can, what one's contribution to that craft or art will be—knowing what one's contribution to his people or his time will be.

CARL T. ROWAN

Imagine a newspaperman winning three prestigious journalism awards by the time he is thirty years old. Then imagine him being selected as one of "America's Ten Outstanding Young Men" by the United States Junior Chamber of Commerce and going on to become one of the nation's leading journalists as well as a high government official and diplomat.

This has all happened to Carl T. Rowan, a syndicated columnist in dozens of newspapers across the country. He also is a political commentator on radio and television and is a roving editor for the *Reader's Digest*. His books have received wide critical acclaim.

It all began for Rowan in the little town of Ravenscroft,

Tennessee, where he was born in 1925. After graduating from high school in McMinnville, Tennessee, he attended Tennessee State College in Nashville for one year before joining the United States Navy. At the age of nineteen he became one of the first fifteen Negroes to be commissioned as Navy officers.

Following three years of World War II service, Rowan returned to civilian life and earned a bachelor's degree from Oberlin College in Ohio and a master's in journalism from the University of Minnesota.

In 1948, when it was almost unheard of for a daily newspaper to hire blacks, Rowan joined the staff of the *Minneapolis Tribune*, where he soon established himself as a crack reporter. He covered a number of major news stories, including the visit to the United States of Soviet Premier Nikita Khrushchev, the school desegregation troubles in Little Rock, Arkansas, the U-2 spy plane controversy, the Hungarian uprising, the Suez crisis and the Asian-African conference in Bandung, Indonesia. In 1953 he won the Sigma Delta Chi medallion for "best general reporting" based on his articles about school desegregation court cases. The following year he won the honor again for the "best foreign correspondent," growing out of his coverage of India, and in 1955 he took the same prize for a series of pieces on Southeast Asia and the Bandung conference.

Additional awards were heaped on this tireless and enterprising newsman. He also has garnered the citation by the National Urban League for distinguished reporting of national and world affairs and for "unselfish leadership in fostering better race relations." The University of Minnesota regents have given him their "distinguished achievement award," and in 1964 he was elected to the board of trustees of his alma mater, Oberlin College. In 1968 Rowan was chosen the 1968 Elijah P. Lovejoy Fellow of Colby College, an award given each year to a newspaperman of integrity. It was named after an Illinois weekly publisher who was killed in the nineteenth century by a mob that invaded his newspaper office.

Such achievement eventually came to the attention of President John F. Kennedy, who in 1961 appointed Carl Rowan Assistant Secretary of State for Public Affairs. He was subsequently United States ambassador to Finland and a member of this country's delegation to the United Nations, and he served as director of the United States Information Agency before returning to journalism in 1965.

When he left government service, Rowan became a columnist for the Chicago *Daily News*, which syndicates his column in about 180 newspapers through the Publishers-Hall Syndicate, one of five syndicates which offered to handle his writing. Rowan said at the time: "It was a good feeling to [be offered] the kind of money I never thought was in journalism fifteen years ago. But I had a feeling of satisfaction beyond what it meant to my personal pocketbook. It meant that Negroes, like white Americans, can leave government and face economic opportunity commensurate with what they know and are prepared to deliver. This has not always been so. The Negro who got a good job in government was prepared to make it his home. But my old profession came through beautifully, and I hope that this indicates we've reached a new day."

In 1970 Rowan achieved a breakthrough that many thought would never be possible. He was allowed into South Africa to report on that nation's apartheid, or segregated policies, and other aspects of its life. Refused permission to visit South Africa in 1956 because he was black, Rowan had to wait only four days for a visa this time. He traveled throughout the country, staying in white hotels, meeting government officials and viewing apartheid at close quarters. He described South Africa as "a nightmare and a dream." He added that it was "the embodiment of fear—more kinds of fear than most societies ever dreamt of" and "a country that lives by the doubts of tomorrow, dies by the injustices of today."

Many, but by no means all, of Rowan's columns relate to the race issue. As a newspaperman and government official of long experience, he is well equipped to write on varied topics and does so. These include foreign policy, domestic matters and social change.

His books include *South of Freedom*, a study of the racial situation in the South, *The Pitiful and the Proud*, about Asia, and *Go South to Sorrow*, an analysis of America's race problems.

WILLIAM J. RASPBERRY

"When I first started writing the column I was quite self-conscious about being black, but eventually I got honest with myself and realized that the most important and fascinating news story of the 1960s was that of race relations."

So said William Raspberry, *Washington Post* columnist, in an interview with an *Editor & Publisher* magazine reporter in 1969. He had been writing the column since 1966, after stints on the *Post*'s copy desk and as a reporter. When Raspberry took it over, the column was called "Potomac Watch" and concerned itself with such metropolitan matters as garbage collection, the operation of the airport and capital sights. He continued this policy for a few months before he realized that as a black he could use the column as a voice for

Washington blacks, who comprise most of the city's population.

Since that time, the column, which now carries only his name on top, offers a special insight into racial issues. He has written about raising achievement in the public school system, discriminatory advertisements and the difficulty blacks have in getting business loans. In one column, he observed: "Now I don't believe that every bank in the District of Columbia has a vice president in charge of discrimination. But the system of standards for long-term borrowing was developed with whites in mind and they happen to work against Negroes." The day the column appeared a black hotel owner who had been vainly trying to get a loan was offered several of them by local banks.

Another column about an organization called "Big Brothers of Washington" resulted in dozens of phone calls from affluent blacks and whites pledging to help slum children.

A native of Okolona, Mississippi, Raspberry attended Indian Central College in Indianapolis and then learned the newspaper business as a reporter, photographer and proofreader on the Indianapolis *Recorder*, a weekly. He was drafted into the Army in April, 1960, shortly after he had been promoted to managing editor.

The draft proved, however, to be a key link in Raspberry's career. The Army sent him to Washington as a public information officer, and it was there that he got the idea of working for the *Post*. When he was discharged he applied to the paper for the job of teletype operator for a new news service the paper was starting. That seemed to be the only opening.

It didn't take *Post* editors long to find out that Raspberry knew little about operating a teletype machine, but they were impressed with his writing ability. They moved him to the obituary section and then to police, court and general assignment reporting. When he was offered the "Potomac Watch" column he at first refused, but *Post* executives persuaded him to try it.

"I don't see myself as a crusader," he has said. "What the column can do is provide graphic illustrations of the nature of the problem, and people brighter than I can figure out the solutions."

To get his illustrations, William Raspberry talks to many people, black and white, in places as widely separated as cocktail parties in big hotels and the Washington ghetto, where he strolls frequently, stopping to chat with laborers, welfare recipients and anyone else who might be the source of an item. His incisive probing and lucid writing style have earned the thirty-six-year-old columnist a bevy of awards, including the Capital Press Club's "Journalist of the Year" in 1965 for his coverage of the Watts riot in Los Angeles. He also has won the Federal Bar Association's Liberty Bell award for his "outstanding community service in promoting responsible citizenship."

Raspberry is a contributing editor to the ABC News evening television newscasts from Washington.

L. F. PALMER, JR.

L. F. "Lu" Palmer is a plain-talking, plain-writing, cigar-chewing reporter who enjoys nothing more than a good argument with his editors if he thinks he's right. The editors of the Chicago *Daily News*, where Palmer works, don't hesitate to argue back if they feel they're right. The result is a mutual respect for each other's opinions, although Palmer wins a lot of the arguments.

Lu Palmer "tells it like it is" whether he is turning out straight news stories or writing his once-a-week column on black affairs which is syndicated in more than one hundred newspapers. The column projects a black point of view, but it is written so clearly that it is easily grasped by both whites and blacks. Palmer produces a black-oriented column out of choice. "The biggest-running story in the nation has been and will continue to be the conflict between black and white America," he explains. "I don't think it's being adequately or honestly covered, and that's why I chose to specialize in it." His columns have sharply examined such subjects as black studies, racism in churches and the Chicago ghetto. When racial conflict erupts he is in the thick of it.

The forty-eight-year-old newsman was born in Newport News, Virginia, and graduated from Virginia Union University with a major in sociology. He next got a master's degree in journalism at Syracuse University and then began work on his Ph.D. at the University of Iowa. But at the same time he had a strong interest in journalism and he became a reporter for the black *Chicago Defender*. In the 1950s he left the newspaper business for a few years and was successively public information officer for Provident Hospital in Chicago and director of the news bureau of Fisk University in Nashville, Tennessee.

When he returned to journalism it was with a white daily, the Chicago *American*, writing general and black community news. Later Palmer was hired away by the Chicago *Daily News*, and his reputation began gaining momentum. He has won several journalism awards, including the Washington, D.C., Capital Press Club's Honor Award, the Chicago Newspaper Guild's Page One Award on two occasions and the Helen Cody Baker Special Media Award. In addition to his writing, Palmer has his own news analysis program, "Lu's Notebook," on four Chicago-area radio stations.

Palmer credits his years on the black *Defender* for his ability to meet fast deadlines in a highly competitive business. "I was way ahead of the white reporters when I joined the Chicago *American*," he said. "Having worked on a black weekly I acquired speed and knowledge of all the different operations on a newspaper. On the *American* I started off on the midnight shift as a rewrite man. The white reporters would jab me in the ribs and say, 'Look, man, you're grinding out too much copy. You're turning in five or six stories, and we're turning in two or three.'

"Well, I was working at my own pace. But I soon realized that the night city editor was dumping all the best stories on me. It kind of made the other fellows jealous. This could have been because I was older than they, but I really think it was due to my previous experience. I believe the black press is about the best training that you can find."

The Chicago reporter is keenly interested in getting young blacks into journalism and has some definite ideas on how this can be accomplished. He advises them to study journalism in college, but at the same time he feels that journalism schools must make adjustments in their curricula "to explore honestly the black and white conflict in the press." Palmer added:

"A young black journalist needs to know what he meets when he comes into a story in which he may be the only black reporter. Let's face it; he's not coming into a normal situation. And if he's covering black news he's really going to have to learn his way around in order to get his stuff in the paper the way he wrote it."

Some journalism schools have introduced courses on covering the racial crisis in America, such as the one taught at

New York University by Thomas A. Johnson of *The New York Times.*

EARL CALDWELL

The right to protect his sources is one of the journalist's most prized privileges. Very often a news source will disclose information to a reporter only on the assurance that he will remain anonymous. The material is printed in the newspaper or broadcast, but without the name of the informant.

Reporters want to protect sources for a simple reason. If an informer's name leaks out, he will no longer trust the journalist who had promised him that it would not. Thus the reporter, who relies on such tips, would be seriously handicapped in his work. Sources demanding anonymity range from underworld figures to high government officials.

In the spring of 1970 this privilege was challenged by the United States government in a case that drew the attention of all segments of the American press. It involved a young black man named Earl Caldwell, a West Coast reporter for *The New York Times.* The Department of Justice subpoenaed Caldwell to appear before a Federal grand jury and produce tapes and notes of his interviews with Black Panther leaders. When the reporter refused, he was served with a contempt citation which could have sent him to jail.

But Caldwell appealed to a higher court, paving the way for a landmark decision that may affect journalism for years to come. The Federal Ninth Circuit Court of Appeals in November, 1970, upheld Caldwell's position and ordered the charges against him dropped. The court also issued a new definition of a newspaperman's privilege which stated that Federal officers must make a clear showing of "compelling and overriding national interest that cannot be served by al-

ternate means" before they can issue subpoenas for newsmen's files.

"The very concept of a free press requires that the news
media be accorded a measure of autonomy," the three-mem-
ber judges panel declared.

Earl Caldwell said of the decision: "I was prepared to go
to jail and stay. It's not just my victory; it's an essential victory for the whole communications business."

And so it was. Caldwell was supported by his own newspaper, the *Times*, and by the *Washington Post, Newsweek*
magazine, the Author's Guild, the American Civil Liberties
Union and thousands of newsmen and women who realized
that their own futures were at stake in the case. A special
plea in Caldwell's behalf was made by sixty-six black journalists from media throughout the United States. The group
declared in a full-page newspaper ad:

. . . We feel that he [Caldwell] was subpoenaed because it was felt that, as a black man, he had special
access to information in the black community. Thus the
role of every black news man and woman has been put
into question—Are we government agents? Will we reveal confidential sources if subpoenaed? Can our employers turn over our files, notes or tapes if we object?
. . . It is of utmost importance that our position as black
men and women in the news business be reaffirmed in
the black community. We do not intend to be used as
spies, informers or undercover agents by anybody—
period! We will protect our confidential sources, using
every means at our disposal. . . .

Implied in the statement was the knowledge that some
black reporters for white media have been accused in the

black community of being spies or "Uncle Toms." It's obvious that news sources in the ghetto would be reluctant to give reporters information if they knew the Justice Department could compel them to reveal their contacts.

The government has appealed the decision to the United States Supreme Court. Meanwhile, Earl Caldwell is carrying out his duties in the *Times* San Francisco office, where he was assigned in 1969, after serving that paper for two years as a metropolitan reporter in New York City.

He began his newspaper career on the *Progress* in his hometown of Clearfield, Pennsylvania, after graduating from the University of Buffalo. His next job was on the Lancaster (Pennsylvania) *Intelligencer-Journal,* covering both sports and general assignment. Later he worked for the *New York Herald Tribune* and the New York *Post* before joining the *Times.*

Only thirty-three years old at the time of this writing, Earl Caldwell appears to be a reporter with a bright future.

WARREN BROWN

When Warren Brown began working for the New Orleans *States-Item* in 1970, he had completed a long round trip. That's where he was born and grew up, but it took a few years in New York to convince him that New Orleans was where he wanted to practice his trade. He reports on the black community through choice because of "the fact that black news nowadays is greatly affected by what transpires in white America and vice versa."

The twenty-three-year-old reporter was born into a family in which education had a prominent place. His father, Daniel T. Brown, Sr., was a biology and chemistry teacher in the local public high schools for thirty years. His mother, Lillian, was a business school graduate. Warren and his five brothers and sisters were sent to black Catholic schools on the theory that "they were better than black public schools and equal to white public schools."

Warren entered Xavier College of Louisiana in 1965, majoring in English education on the strength of his father's advice that "only rich white people major in liberal arts, and they don't need jobs." There were no journalism courses at Xavier, but he edited the campus newspaper. He recalls that what little journalism he got was from his white adviser on the newspaper, Dorothy Brown. "She was good and very dedicated," Brown added.

In 1969 he entered the Columbia University Graduate School of Journalism, and that summer he worked as an intern at *Newsday*, getting encouragement from Stanley Asimov, then assistant managing editor. From *Newsday*, Brown went to *The New York Times* as a news clerk, a position given young aspirants for reporting jobs. The *Times* experience, according to Brown, did a great deal toward rounding out his education in journalism.

"I became aware of what reporting and journalism was all about one Sunday while working on the desk.

"Dave Jones, the National Desk editor, wanted to reach one of his men in Atlanta. He ordered me to call him.

"I dialed the man's number. The phone kept ringing."

" 'Nobody home,' I told Jones."

" 'How do you know?' Jones asked."

" 'Nobody answered,' I said."

" 'Then how do you know if no one's home if no one answered?' he asked, and the lesson went on from there."

Despite the value of his training at the *Times*, Brown reasoned that it would take years to move up through the ranks on a paper of that size and magnitude.

Currently, Brown is continuing his learning process at the *States-Item* and "moving in the right direction."

"The right direction for blacks in journalism," he added, "is towards providing more access to the media for those persons who have been historically deprived of that access. These persons are blacks, poor whites and other so-called minority-group members."

Asked how he would advise young persons thinking about journalism, Warren Brown replied:

"I don't like to give advice to those who are not much younger than I am. However, I would urge aspiring journalists, black and white, to read as much as possible. Nothing is as disgusting as an illiterate reporter.

"For blacks in particular, I would urge them to beware of allowing their education to alienate them from their people. There is power in the community, and right now, regardless of who they intend to work for or what type or phase of journalism they intend to enter, they'd better remember what community they belong to."

TED POSTON

Several years ago two cars were speeding along a Florida road. The front auto contained Ted Poston, black reporter for the New York *Post*. In the car behind were four or five Ku Klux Klan members bent on catching Poston. "I knew if they got me it meant the end," he recalled. "But luckily my car was faster than theirs."

Such incidents have been quite common in the newspaper life of Poston. Once, when he was covering a story in Alabama for the New York *Amsterdam News*, he was roughed up by a band of hoodlums. The only thing that saved him from worse harm was the phony preacher's identification he carried with him. When the *Post* assigned him to the Montgomery bus boycotts in 1955, his editor asked him to phone every night to assure him that he was still alive.

Despite these hazards, Ted Poston doesn't sidestep any stories in the South or any other potentially dangerous spot. In fact, he fights with his editors to cover such events because he is qualified and because as a black and a Southerner he feels he has an obligation to go into trouble areas.

Poston became a *Post* reporter in 1937, long before it was stylish to hire blacks on white newspapers. He had begun his newspaper career on his family's paper in Hopkinsville, Kentucky, where he was born in 1906.

"Back in 1922," he said, "we had a Negro weekly called the Hopkinsville *Contender*, owned and operated by my father and my two brothers. I ran the copy to the printer."

When the paper proved too militant for Hopkinsville, it was moved to Nashville, Tennessee, and then to Detroit. "Speech there was a little freer for us," Poston said.

Ted Poston eventually left the paper for Tennessee State College, graduating in 1928. Shortly after, he caught a cattle boat from Savannah, Georgia, to New York, where his brother, Ulysses, was a campaign worker for Alfred E. Smith, Democratic candidate for president that year. Ulysses got Ted a $150-a-week job on one of the campaign papers. "It took me twenty years to get that high again," Poston said. When the Democrats lost, Ted Poston went to work as a dining car waiter on the Pennsylvania Railroad but managed to write a regular column at the same time for the black *Pittsburgh Courier*. During the stock market crash of 1929, Poston got his first full-time newspaper job on the *Amsterdam News*, becoming city editor five years later.

He started at the *Post* as a space rate writer, but a combination of luck and quick thinking got him on the regular staff. As he was leaving the subway one night he saw a white man being chased by a group of blacks, who already had beaten him severely. The newsman shoved the victim into a phone booth and then persuaded his attackers to leave. It turned out that the man was a process server who had tried to serve a warrant on the late Father Devine, an act which outraged his disciples. Poston got an exclusive story on the incident and a steady job. He was the first black to work full-time for a New York daily. During World War II, while on leave from the *Post*, Ted Poston served in the Office of War Information in Washington and later as a consultant to Jonathan Daniels, administrative assistant to President Franklin D. Roosevelt. In the years since, he has covered a number of major stories, including investigations into veterans' housing frauds, police graft and the narcotics traffic.

Poston has said that newspapers have a long way to go in hiring blacks as a means of producing better reporting of racial conflicts. Writing in the anthology *Race and the News Media*, he noted:

"The silken curtain between the major northern newspapers and their Negro readers hasn't been noticeably pierced, in my opinion, by the sporadic hiring of a handful of Negroes. Since editors regard their Negro fellow citizens as a monolithic mass that only they, in their superior wisdom, can understand, why should they listen on the big issues to reporters who are themselves part of that mass?"

But Poston said he would rather report the news than offer opinions on it. He says he doesn't want a column because "I can't solve the problems of the world. I would rather report them."

VERNON D. JARRETT

"I don't intend to spend time pointing to isolated black heroes. It is the heroism of the average black human being that I want to dramatize. This is what strikes me every day that I walk through the streets of the ghetto of Chicago."

These are the words of Vernon D. Jarrett in describing his column appearing in the *Chicago Tribune* twice a week. The column, which has gained wide popularity, expresses the problems, hopes and fears of black Chicagoans.

When he began it in 1970, Jarrett already had impressive credentials in journalism and education. He is the producer of the Chicago television program "For Blacks Only," and has been a visiting associate professor of history at Northwestern University. His newspaper experience has included stints as a reporter and feature writer for the *Chicago Defender,* the *Pittsburgh Courier* and the Associated Negro Press. In addition, he has written numerous radio shows on the black experience and black events throughout the world.

Born in Saulsbury, Tennessee, in 1921, Jarrett graduated from Knoxville College with a degree in history and sociology. He later attended Northwestern and the Universities of Kansas City and Chicago, studying television production and urban sociology.

Besides his writing, teaching and broadcasting, Vernon Jarrett finds time for civic activities. He is vice-president of the Chicago Citizens Schools Committee, an organization devoted to improving public schools. He also serves on the board of the Chicago Association for Theatre, YMCA units and other groups.

ERNEST JOHNSTON, JR.

Ernie Johnston, a *New York Post* reporter, was one of the "front-line" troops during the Newark race riot in 1967. Then a newsman for the Newark *Star-Ledger,* he was on the street day after day, interviewing everyone he could while battles were raging around him.

That baptism of fire was not the last tough situation into which he has been thrust. As a general assignment reporter for the *Post,* he has covered a number of metropolitan conflicts, including a long, bitter struggle over who was to run a neighborhood school—community leaders or the central board of education. Through all these situations, Johnston has managed to preserve his cool. He puts his philosophy plainly: "As I see it, a black reporter is a reporter first. I call them as I see them. I try to do the best professional job I can."

The thirty-two-year-old journalist spends whatever time he can in getting young blacks interested in journalism. "Some black kids," he said, "have never seen a reporter. They're not being motivated in high school toward a journalism career. There are a lot of black youths who are dying to become reporters or news broadcasters. Why let this talent go to waste?"

Johnston covers mostly black news through choice. Often, he will stand away from his reporter's role to help ghetto groups become represented in the media. This may mean aiding them in setting up press conferences or advising them on such media matters as deadlines and news requirements.

Ernie Johnston is a native of Roanoke Rapids, North Carolina. He attended the Agricultural Technical State University at Greensboro in his home state and later served in the United States Army. He began his newspaper years on the black *Journal & Guide* in Norfolk, Virginia, and then moved to the *Star-Ledger.*

WILLIAM J. DRUMMOND

The widely held assumption that only black reporters should cover riots and other ghetto stories is challenged by William

Drummond, twenty-six-year-old reporter for the *Los Angeles Times*.

It is understandable that any Negro hired onto a big daily will consider himself lucky and not complain if he gets the race beat. One reason for the silence is that racial coverage is an important assignment in which there is a great deal of interest and thus a guarantee to the reporter of plentiful exposure. Another reason is that a Negro reporter doubtless feels secure with the race beat because, by dint of his birth, he is an expert, or should be, and he will have easy rapport with sources who are either Negroes or persons used to dealing with them. Third, behind all is a feeling of protectiveness: *No white man could possibly give us as sympathetic treatment as I can; he just would not understand.*

Nevertheless, the terms of this arrangement are a limitation—on editor and reporter. The suspicion that an editor's interest lies in the external man, rather than in the whole man, could prevent a reporter from keeping the faith in his profession.

Drummond, who has covered a multitude of black and general stories, believes that white reporters "who know their business" have been as successful as their black counterparts in reporting racial affairs. He added that a white newsman once told him: "The most important thing is not to be taken for a cop. If you walk up to a guy who is burning down a building and you're wearing a helmet and flak jacket, he might clobber you. But if you're dressed normally, he'll probably tell you why he's burning the building down."

On the *Times*, Bill Drummond has interviewed many

militants in his coverage of such movements as the Black
Panthers and the street people. He also has done a number
of stories on prison problems and police-community relations. In one piece headlined "Blue Denim Jungle: Prison
Race Trouble," he wrote:

> Racial conflict has struck Soledad prison in recent
> months with as much heat and fury as the reckless
> winds that blow through the fertile lettuce bowl of the
> Salinas Valley.
>
> Correctional officers there work in pairs now, after
> two white guards patrolling alone were killed. Their
> deaths came after another white guard shot three black
> prisoners to death during a racial fight last January 13.
>
> But Soledad prison is not unique. A *Times* survey of
> the major state prisons . . . found that a potential for
> racial violence boils just beneath a fragile surface. . . .

William Drummond had journalism on his mind at an
early age. A native of Oakland, California, he attended that
city's McClymonds High School, noted for producing a number of black athletes, including Bill Russell, Frank Robinson,
Vada Pinson and Wendell Hayes.

After graduating with honors in journalism from the University of California at Berkeley and with high honors from
the Columbia University Graduate School of Journalism
(M.A.), Drummond went to work for the Louisville (Kentucky) *Courier-Journal*, specializing in covering the war on
poverty and race relations. He moved to the *Los Angeles
Times* in 1967. Drummond was rewarded for his reportorial
excellence by being made his paper's bureau chief in New
Delhi, India.

WILLIAM ARTHUR HILLIARD

"We simply appointed a city editor, not a black city editor. Just the best man."

This is how a Portland *Oregonian* executive described the promotion of Bill Hilliard, a black newsman, who had joined the paper in 1952 as a copy boy. He became the first black to be named a city editor of a major American daily.

Hilliard got the job because of his high competence as a journalist. He had served as sports reporter, church editor, general assignment man and picture editor before being named assistant city editor in 1962.

A graduate of the University of the Pacific, Hilliard was originally hired by the *Oregonian* (circulation 245,000) because he was black. After the Watts riot in California, however, Bill Hilliard received a number of offers from other newspapers which were belatedly trying to get blacks on their staffs. He decided to stay with the *Oregonian* after his editor told him that there was nothing to stop him from having a good future there. Two years later he did an outstanding job of directing the coverage of racial outbreaks in Portland. Both sides credited him with being fair and impartial.

OVIE CARTER

Ovie Carter, a twenty-five-year-old black photographer for the *Chicago Tribune*, was concerned about drug use, particularly among young addicts. He wanted to shoot a picture story about the drug scene. When the picture editor saw the photos in November, 1970, he was so impressed that he went to editor Clayton Kirkpatrick with an idea that they be used as a layout for a photo editorial. Kirkpatrick agreed, and the pictures were used one day in the space normally devoted to editorials. Later, the spread was featured in *Editor & Publisher* magazine.

The photographs pulled no punches. They consisted of a grim sequence showing how a young person starts with amphetamine or barbiturate pills and graduates to heroin. One picture depicted a shadowy drug pusher making a sale on a dark street. Another revealed an addict shooting heroin into his arm. The caption read: ". . . The buyer risks death because he never knows the potency of the heroin." The final picture was that of a graveyard, with this caption: "Often the trip ends here, after a life of misery, filled with crime to obtain money for the habit."

Little more than a year before, Ovie Carter was working as a lab man in the *Tribune*'s photo department. He had gone there after studying for a year at a Chicago photography school. A native of Indianola, Mississippi, he was educated in St. Louis and at the Forest Park Community College. He spent a year in the Air Force, getting a medical discharge in 1967.

Carter is a member of the Black Journalists Association and the Chicago Press-Photographers Association. One of his off-duty activities is teaching underprivileged children who are interested in photography.

DAVID L. JACKSON

According to David L. Jackson, reporter for the *Detroit News*, the black reporter has two roles in journalism.

"First and foremost," he said, "he must be a professional and handle any type of assignments handed out. Secondly, since he is a Negro, he should be better able to interpret activities in the black community. He should be able to understand what is going on without spending a lot of time on background information."

Jackson has fulfilled both roles for two newspapers. The thirty-one-year-old reporter went on the staff of the Harrisburg (Pennsylvania) *Patriot-News* after graduating in journalism from Temple University. In Harrisburg, the state capital, he covered local government and school boards. At the *Detroit News*, his assignments have included the Detroit City Council, county affairs and politics. He was on the campaign trail of candidates for the United States Senate and for governor of Michigan.

"My advice to anyone entering the business, black or white, would be the same," he asserted. "Concentrate on grammar and spelling and take liberal arts courses to acquaint yourself with a variety of subjects.

"Today, many newspapers are hiring black persons without much formal training because of the shortage of minority workers in the field. However, once the law of supply and demand evens out, only the capable black writers will remain in the profession. This is why it is important for Negro writers to think of themselves as professional journalists who just happen to be black."

HENRI E. WITTENBERG

It is rare when a newspaper employee moves from the circulation to the editorial department. It is rarer still when the employee is black. Henri Wittenberg achieved the change-over at the *Detroit News*, where he is a city-side reporter at the age of forty-one.

In the latter part of 1968, Wittenberg was a district manager for the *News*. The position entailed handling delivery to subscribers, collections and supervising carriers. In the years before, he had been a counselor to prisoners for the United States Department of Justice, an assistant terminal manager for the Greyhound Corporation and an administrative assistant to a Ford Motor Company plant superintendent. He had attended Wilberforce and Northwestern Universities for two and one-half years.

Restless and convinced that he was in the wrong slot, Wittenberg resigned from the *News* circulation job. The circulation and editorial departments were on the same floor, and he decided to stop in at the latter before leaving the building. He had always wanted to be a writer, and there seemed to be nothing to lose in applying for a reporter's position.

The editors were not encouraging. One told Wittenberg that the *News* usually hired reporters only after they had had years of experience on smaller papers. They also were a little more than astonished that an applicant should emerge from the circulation department.

But Wittenberg got one break—the only one he needed, as it turned out. Columbia University's Graduate School of Journalism was offering a ten-week summer session for aspiring journalists in the summer of 1969. The managing editor of the *News* told Wittenberg that if he successfully completed the course he would be taken on as a reporter. He did, and the *News* kept its word.

Henri Wittenberg is convinced that the print medium is the best way to circulate ideas. "When a person is seen on television, a quick glance is usually involved. If you rush from another room to hear a statement that interests you, there is a good chance you might miss the meaning of what was said. However, when words are printed and circulated, they can be passed on and referred to over and over again.

Printed stories are saved and brought out again in every walk of life."

As a reporter, Henri Wittenberg is familiar with the term "objectivity" and the reverence in which it is held in the Establishment media. But he doesn't subscribe to the theory —at least, not in the traditional sense.

"To me, objectivity is a joke word," Wittenberg said. "I feel that I can cover any situation and bring back what was said and done without attaching my own feelings to a story. I know I can be fair in a story, but when I knock the objectivity theory, I have in mind going into an area where some woman of my race has never worn a decent pair of shoes, eaten in a decent restaurant or held any real hopes for the future. I cannot feel objective about a public official —such as a United States senator who belongs to an exclusive club of one hundred—receiving untold benefits without much criticism, while some woman who is widowed, receives financial assistance and wants to keep her family together must be subjected to many degrading questions in order to get $100."

Wittenberg said that the stories that he most enjoys covering are those in which "someone has been helped." He declared that he has little interest in writing a column or opinion piece; instead he prefers "getting good information and presenting it for others to form opinions."

His counsel to young blacks looking toward a journalism career is as follows:

"Listen. Learn to listen to everyone—young, old, educated, rich, poor, those who can barely sign their names. Talk is easy, but every human has something to convey if a person will listen. Underestimate no one; never talk down to another."

He also recommended extensive reading but observed that the quest for knowledge should be in the areas where the young person is weakest. "Read up on subjects about which you feel you lack interest," he said. "And, as much as possible, strive to make every person you meet a real contact. This includes people in community, political, religious, educational and scientific work."

Henri Wittenberg knows why he wanted to be a reporter in the first place. "I have a very strong interest in people," he explained. "I also have a long-time desire to know what makes them tick. I have much feeling for blacks in America because my paternal grandmother was a slave. However, I have strong feelings for all human beings. Differences in tongue, custom and costume are not important to me."

OTHER BLACK NEWSMEN

There is not room in this book to include all of the black reporters and other editorial personnel on American newspapers. The number of black journalists is not as large as it should be, but it's growing year by year as newspapers and other media recognize the necessity of having them—not as tokens but as fully contributing members of the staff.

Among other black newsmen are Gerald V. Jackson, of the Boston *Herald-Traveler*, and George E. Hardin and Rodney E. Whitaker, of the Memphis *Commercial Appe*al. Jackson, aged forty-six, a World War II veteran, started newspapering on two black weeklies before becoming a general assignment reporter for the *Herald-Traveler*. He attended Boston University and Emerson College in Boston.

Hardin is a copy reader, a newsroom specialist who reads the reporters' copy for accuracy and style and then writes a headline for the story. Copy editors rarely get a by-line or cover events, but they nevertheless perform one of the most important functions on a newspaper.

A native of Memphis, Hardin worked on black papers before being employed by the *Commercial Appeal* in 1966. He attended the New York Institute of Photography and Tennessee State University.

Rodney Whitaker, a reporter, joined the newspaper in 1967 after attending Le Moyne College in Memphis.

Still other working black newspapermen are Hugh Wyatt, New York *Daily News*; Claude Lewis, *Philadelphia Bulletin*; Jesse Walker and Les Matthews, New York *Amsterdam News*; Mel Watkins, *The New York Times*; and Donald Franklin, *St. Louis Post-Dispatch*.

4/Blacks on the Wire Services

Most American newspapers depend on the wire services for national and international news. These services, also called press associations, maintain bureaus throughout the world. News gathered and written by their reporters is sent to customer newspapers and broadcast stations by means of leased telegraph lines. A report on an assassination in Turkey, for example, can be flashed world-wide in a few seconds.

The two largest wire services are the Associated Press and United Press International, both American organizations. Their editorial employees have two words hammered into them constantly: speed and accuracy. The UPI motto is "a deadline every minute." The press associations have no newspapers of their own, but their customers are always going to press or on the air somewhere around the world. UPI and AP men and women are taught early in the game to be fast as well as sure that the story is correct. Any error would turn up in hundreds of different newspapers and on broadcast stations throughout the globe.

Blacks have not been hired on the wire services in significant numbers, but this wall, too, is cracking. Black reporters for both AP and UPI have shown by their performances that they can meet the demands of these news operations. Here are some of them:

AUSTIN SCOTT

Investigative reporting is, for many newsmen, a highly satisfying way to make a living. The work is hard, but the results often make front-page headlines—to say nothing of the reputation of the reporter.

Austin Scott, a bearded black reporter who rides a motorcycle for recreation, is a prime example of the investigating journalist. He is a member of an eleven-man special assignment team operating out of the Washington office of the Associated Press. Scott and his colleagues have uncovered stories that have appeared in papers around the nation, bearing such headlines as:

TWO CLINICS PAID MILLIONS IN MEDICARE
"GHOST" OIL FOUNDATIONS AVOID MILLIONS IN TAXES
RIOT CLEANUP FUNDS FUNDING OTHER THINGS
FIRM LINKED TO MAFIA HOLDS DEFENSE CONTRACT
CHICKENS BEARING CANCER VIRUS OK'D BY U.S. PANEL
GOVERNMENT FILES KEEP MOUNTAINS OF DATA ON CITIZENS

Time magazine appraised the efforts of the AP group with this observation: "The success of AP's Special Assignment team demonstrates a journalistic truth that the daily press still too often ignores: in an age of complexity, depth is often more necessary than speed. This kind of reporting may be more expensive and more exacting, but its result is also more satisfying."

Austin Scott has been with the Associated Press since he graduated from Stanford University in 1961 with a degree in journalism. His first three years with AP were spent in the Sacramento, California, bureau. He was transferred to New York in 1964, when he began to cover the civil rights

field. From 1964 to 1969, he helped to report almost every
ghetto riot, including those in Detroit, Newark, Cleveland,
Harlem, Buffalo and Tampa. Between crisis stories he
covered conventions of civil rights and black power groups.
He also was on the AP staff that reported the Republican
and Democratic presidential conventions of 1968.

In 1969, after spending seven weeks writing a report on
San Francisco State College for the National Commission on
the Causes and Prevention of Violence, Scott was assigned
to a number of campus uprisings. Later that year he was
awarded a Nieman Fellowship to study urban affairs and
American political history at Harvard University.

JOHN L. TAYLOR

As acting night manager of UPI's Chicago bureau, John
Taylor has a big and complex job. He oversees and prepares
part of the wire service's news report for morning newspapers in the Midwest. Some of the dispatches go over UPI
circuits to the rest of the nation and the world.

Before he took a desk job, Taylor was considered an outstanding feature writer. One of his stories (written with
H. D. Quigg) concerned the life of a poverty-stricken family
in Harlem. The piece was so effective that UPI included it
in *Selections 1968*, a booklet of the press association's best
stories for that year. The article, called "One Day, One
Family, One Slum," begins:

NEW YORK—Cold spring rain wets the car tops and
the streets. On an avenue in Harlem, hand-lettered
window signs are prominent in the shop fronts. "Jesus
Saves" . . . "U.S. Out of Vietnam" . . . "Hell no,
Black won't go."

One of New York's new buses, equipped with panels for advertising on the outside, mutters along the avenue. The panels on one side have not been sold yet, and they bear two of the phrases of whimsical urging that the ad agency uses to fill unused space.

"Dream a butterfly," the bus advises. And: "Explore a Street."

At this place, and in this time, that is a strangely cruel combination of commands. Anyone who explores a side street here is not going to dream a butterfly. He is going to dream a cockroach or a rat.

It is a gray and cold late afternoon. You're guided down a side street by a neighborhood worker who warns you not to be surprised at anything you might see. The block seems quiet enough. A candy store, real estate office, barber shop, apartment houses, a public school.

You enter the apartment building that is home for the family that has consented to let a stranger share an ordinary day with them. In the downstairs hallway a group of about ten, including several teen-agers, are shooting craps—the smooth hardstone floor is alive with $5 and $10 bills and several pair of dice. . . .

The air in the elevator to the seventh floor is heavy with the smell of urine. It's a little, self-operating elevator that rises very slowly. The corridor of this top floor has a depressed spot. In it is a pool of water of undetermined origin. Beyond that lies the apartment door of our family. . . .

John Taylor joined United Press International in 1967 after working as a writer, advertising salesman and city editor for the *Kansas City Call*, a black weekly. He was weekend night manager for UPI in Chicago before his promotion. A native of New Madrid, Missouri, he was graduated with a degree in journalism from Lincoln University in Jefferson City, Missouri.

UPI, in conjunction with the Ford Foundation, sponsored a journalism internship program for fifteen minority-group youths from 1969 to 1971. The internees got their basic training in UPI bureaus and then were placed in other news positions after a year. One of the trainees, Lawrence M. Bryant, aged thirty, was working as a free-lance reporter for a Washington, D.C., radio station when he was hired. He had completed one year at Southern Illinois University and continued his education at American University in Washington while interning at UPI's bureau in the capital. The following is a supervisor's report of Bryant's performance on the internship:

Bryant's interview and his application indicated a great desire to write and inform the public by writing. Although he had done some writing for school publications, it was unpolished. But he improved quickly and a story on "Black English," hunched, researched and written by Bryant, was widely published and brought him commendation. In addition to routine but important desk work, he covered the Washington beat from White House to Capitol and other government news sources. He showed more interest in radio writing and was given intensive training on the Washington bureau radio desk. Grant Dillman, UPI's bureau manager, said, "Bryant was one of the most promising young men ever to pass through the Washington bureau." Bryant left the training program March 21, 1970, to accept a job with

WTTG-TV where his working hours would permit him to continue his studies.

Another trainee, Carolyn Bowers, aged twenty-two, was accepted into the program after graduating with a B.A. in English from Morgan State College, Baltimore, Maryland. Her eighth-grade elementary school teacher had told her, "Carolyn, you should consider journalism." Other teachers had complimented her on her poems and essays. Her UPI supervisor reported:

"Carolyn admitted being bewildered during the first few weeks of her training. But she quickly adjusted to the operational pattern. Most of her early work was on the New York Local Desk. She handled desk duties, did some rewrite and was assigned to feature stories. Her progress was swift. On March 16, 1970, she was transferred to the Feature Department. Her progress continues at a quickening pace, and her by-lined stories appear regularly on the UPI news wires and in the mailed services."

UPI Women's Editor Gay Pauley said of Miss Bowers: "[She] came into the women's department on March 16. I don't know, now, how we made it before her arrival.

"I turned her loose at first just developing ideas, some of her own, some from others around the department as we talked. She did an excellent job on the new boom in home sewing, likewise on the boom in wigs. . . . Her roundup for the bridal page on the high cost of loving [getting married] was, with bureau cooperation, excellently handled."

Carolyn Bowers later was hired as a reporter by the New York *Daily News*.

Harold Blumenfeld, director of the training project, said that of the fifteen interns, only one dropped out because he couldn't make the grade. UPI found permanent jobs for ten of the trainees, and four are still working in the program. The fifteen had come from such diverse backgrounds as college, shipping clerk jobs, the armed services and the streets of New York. Asked to evaluate the internship, one male trainee replied that he thought the program was an excellent opportunity for himself and other young blacks, but he felt that supervisors weren't critical enough during the early stages of the internship. "You shouldn't treat us as freaks or fragile eggs," he commented. "You should be critically tough when it is necessary."

ROLAND DRAUGHON

The South Carolina National Guard inadvertently helped Roland Draughon get his present job in the Philadelphia bureau of the Associated Press.

In 1969 Draughon was public relations director for Voorhees College, a tiny black institution in Denmark, South Carolina. During a bitterly cold winter a dispute broke out between students and the administration. A warning was issued that if the administration building was not cleared by 5 P.M., students would take it over. There also was a threat against the life of the college president.

The administration ordered the college closed and the students to leave the campus. But about a hundred students refused to be bussed out. They spent the night on the quadrangle, chanting, "Hell no! We won't go!"

Meanwhile, in his trailer home, Roland Draughon was trying to catch a little sleep after working an eighteen-hour day as a link between the press and the administration.

"The wire services and newspapers around the country were giving me fits," Draughon recalled. "I wanted to help them, but there was nothing I could do. They had a duty to perform, but I was under orders.

" 'We will have a statement shortly,' I would tell them. 'As soon as I get a statement, I will call you.'

"It was a line I always hated. It took the administration a full day of meetings to come up with an eighty-word statement saying the school had been closed and all the students had been ordered to leave."

Draughon had just dozed off when guardsmen began hammering on his door with rifle butts. He learned later that the soldiers had already wrecked part of the campus, searching for students.

"They didn't believe I was an employee of the college," Draughon remembers. "They made me stand barefooted in the ice while they handcuffed my hands behind my back and marched me to the administration building." There, college officials confirmed that the stocky public relations aide was on the payroll.

Nevertheless, the guards ordered him off the campus. "They wouldn't even let me go back to my trailer and pack my belongings," Draughon said.

He never went back to Voorhees. In April of that year he joined the AP news staff in Philadelphia, and began a career he had wanted for some years. He previously had turned down a job offered by a Midwestern newspaper.

"The managing editor wrote me that he wanted to increase the number of black staffers," Draughon explained. "I did not want, and do not want, to be saddled with black stories all the time. I want to have the ability to do everything. As a black, I realize that in many cases I can get information from black sources who might not communicate with a white reporter. And the black side of stories involving race needs to be told from the black point of view to put it in perspective. I want to handle these stories. But I want to do other things, too."

He has. In little more than a year, Draughon has had his by-line over a number of major stories on AP's national news wire. Some of the pieces—the plenary session of the Conference of Revolutionary Peoples, a Black Panther–sponsored gathering, and a convention of the Fraternal Organization of Black Policemen being two examples—were on black affairs. But he also has written about state and Federal courts, the financial troubles of the Penn Central Railroad, state government, a new method of marketing automobiles and just about everything else that occurs in the area covered by the Associated Press's Philadelphia bureau.

"I love the job and am continuing to learn," Draughon said. One of his recent assignments took him to the Mississippi Delta country as part of a two-man news team. The other member was Jules Loh, of AP News features in New York, a white native of Mississippi. Together, they chronicled the racial and social changes that have taken place there since James Meredith became the first black to attend the University of Mississippi.

"It was a fascinating experience," Draughon remarked. "I had never been there before, and naturally I was a little apprehensive about what I might encounter. There is still discrimination, more subtle and not as flagrant as before. The registration of black voters has increased their political power, but there still is a fear and a long way to go."

Roland Draughon traces his interest in journalism back to his high school days in Dunn, North Carolina, where he was editor of the school paper and class valedictorian. He was born in 1947 in Fayetteville, North Carolina.

In 1965 his family moved to Willow Grove, Pennsylvania, a Philadelphia suburb. His parents wanted him to become a doctor, and Draughon began to comply with their wishes, although with some misgivings. He entered Johnson C. Smith University, a black college in Charlotte, North Carolina, taking a premed course.

"It wasn't long before I realized I was barking up the wrong career," Draughon said. "One semester of zoology, and I knew medicine was not for me." He switched his major to English, worked for both the yearbook and the campus newspaper and made the dean's list.

Draughon would like to see more blacks pursue a news career. He feels that one problem is that many blacks are unprepared because of their early training.

"English has been a traditionally tough language for many blacks because of the poor quality of education many get," he asserted. "Many of the teachers are ill prepared, and this doesn't help the students. They just don't have the skills."

Also, he feels, there is a tendency on the part of many black college students who want to write to believe they can crash into the field as novelists, playwrights or poets.

"They have seen the successes of blacks in these fields and are not aware of similar successes among newspaper or news service jobs, so they just don't try," he said.

As for Draughon, he plans to stay with journalism. "This digging and getting into the meaning of things, not just going into the surface matter, is one of the reasons I find AP work so exciting," he summed up.

5 / Ladies of the Press

For a number of years women found it tough to get jobs on newspapers. There was the occasional "sob sister" who wrote emotionally about murder, mayhem and sex, but she was a rarity in the city room. Most women seeking writing or reporting assignments were relegated to the women's pages, where they turned out conventional stories on engagements, weddings, parties and social chitchat.

The latter half of the twentieth century saw a dramatic change in this situation. During World War II thousands of male newsmen went into the armed services or became combat correspondents. Desperate for help, home-town editors hired women in unprecedented numbers. Many were journalism graduates, while others had had no previous training or experience. In most cases, the editors were delighted with the results. They found that the ladies could do just about any task as well as men—and in some cases better. The door had finally swung open for women journalists.

Today, women reporters are commonplace. Some newspapers, especially suburban ones, have almost as many women as men on the city side. This can be confirmed by reading by-lines in various dailies.

Black women, of course, had an even more difficult time finding newspaper employment on white newspapers. The few blacks who did get such jobs in the 1940s and 1950s were, in almost all cases, male. But this has changed, too.

Most metropolitan dailies have at least one black woman on the news side and some have more. They include *The New York Times*, the *Chicago Tribune*, the *San Francisco Examiner*, the *St. Louis Post-Dispatch, Newsday* and others. The following sketches do not purport to be a complete compilation of black newswomen, but are merely meant to be representative.

CHARLAYNE HUNTER

In the fall of 1961, a tall, young girl named Charlayne Hunter made history the hard way. She was one of the first two black students to be integrated into the University of Georgia. White students rioted outside the dormitory where she lived, and bottles and bricks were hurled through her window. Girls living in the room above her pounded on the floor night after night. The experience left her so emotionally and physically exhausted that she had trouble staying awake in classes. But she survived the ordeal and went on to get her bachelor's degree in journalism.

Since that time Charlayne Hunter has become a top reporter for *The New York Times*, where she made history again by being chosen to head the newspaper's first bureau in Harlem. Her by-lined stories on the black community appear regularly in the *Times*, and she also writes magazine articles.

Before joining the *Times* in 1969, Miss Hunter had been a news reporter with WRC-TV in Washington, D.C., a "Talk of the Town" writer for the *New Yorker* magazine and a manuscript editor of *Transaction* magazine. She later wrote an article for the latter publication on the Poor People's March to Washington.

As a television reporter, Miss Hunter met another form of

discrimination. There were then so few blacks in TV news
departments that news sources would sometimes ignore her
and address themselves to her white technical crew, assuming that she was a clerk or office girl. Miss Hunter and other
black reporters occasionally encounter such reaction today,
but less and less so.

One of Miss Hunter's colleagues on the *Times* has called
her a "gifted reporter and writer" who asks questions with
"patient sensitivity and deliberateness." Her fight against
prejudice has left her with some bitterness, but has not affected her high professional skill and competence.

A native of Due West, South Carolina, Miss Hunter spent
a year of elementary school in Anchorage, Alaska, where her
father was an Army chaplain. As a child, some of her summer
vacations were spent at the home of her grandmother in
Harlem. In recalling those periods in a *New Yorker* article,
she wrote that "hallways on that block were darker and more
forbidding than the calaboose back home."

Miss Hunter graduated from high school in Atlanta,
Georgia, and then attended Wayne State University in Detroit for two years before she was admitted to the University
of Georgia on a court order.

A successful reporter herself, Miss Hunter is keenly interested in the welfare of black newsmen and women, especially the younger ones. She has criticized some editors
for not permitting black staffers to use their full capabilities.

"Black reporters," she said, "should be allowed to handle
all kinds of stories, not just black ones. If a black reporter
wants to cover the black community, he should be given the
opportunity. If not, he should be assigned to something else.
There also should be more black editors and copy readers."

Miss Hunter believes that "black reporters must become
revolutionaries—agents of change rather than just agents;

part of the solution. And it can be done, while maintaining a sense of fairness—some prefer objectivity—and ethical correctness, as well.

"Because the most important story of the last decade has undoubtedly been race relations—good ones, bad ones and often none at all—the black reporter should have emerged as one of the most valuable commodities of the news media industry. But his value has been affected by constraints and powerlessness—in both black and white media—and he has become, instead, the most underrated commodity of the industry.

"For the good of all of us—the community, the communications industry, the nation and the black reporter as a black person—that has got to change. For the black reporter has an edge, if not a corner, on the truth market in black communities today."

According to Miss Hunter, a good white reporter may go into the black community and do a fair story, but he is likely to run into problems of credibility with blacks "who feel justifiably betrayed by his bosses, who look like him."

"It's going to be tough, if not impossible," she added, "for him to know from guarded conversations what he might otherwise know if he lived there and didn't need to be told.

"As black reporters, we know where the errors of omission occurred, know that if we had been given the chance all along to write about what we knew, no one would have been surprised at Harlem; Watts, 1965; Newark and Detroit, 1967; Washington, 1968; and hundreds of other ignited cities right up to now. Little of the truth got out in 1964 because if we weren't in black media, we weren't in any media. And if we were in the black media, all too often our stands were modified to suit the advertisers' needs that were not necessarily our own.

"Today, despite the fact that there are a few of us in white media, and a few of us with fuller resources in black media, the news columns and what fills the air rarely reflect our special abilities."

Miss Hunter asserts that black newsmen and women will gain real power only when they are in a position to make or affect editorial decisions—to render judgments and make changes.

Only with rare exception do we have the power to tell the whole truth. And none of that will change until we are greater in number and solidarity of purpose.

Meanwhile, there are other approaches to the problem of enhancing our value and improving the quality of news coverage in the community. For too long, the black reporter has been unwilling or unable to accept the responsibility of being part of the solution. As a result, he has allowed his blackness to be used and unwittingly has become a part of the problem. While being sent on assignments in the community because he was black, the black reporter responded to the pretenses of his white editors—that being black had nothing to do with his being sent—and came back with reports that were other than black in perspective.

And when the reports came out, the situation was something other than what was in print or on the air; it was not the institution that suffered but the credibility of the black reporter. The community, after all, is not looking for handouts. It is looking for honest people who will look at it honestly—its blemishes, its beauty—and then tell the truth.

Miss Hunter herself refuses to be typecast as either a

martyr or as a symbol. To a magazine writer doing a series on her she said: "I'm too young to have already done the most important things in my life. I don't want to be an ideal girl—just a girl."

BETTY WASHINGTON

Some people come into journalism by accident. Others, like Betty Washington, aim for it from the time they are in grammar school. Miss Washington began to take writing seriously in the fifth or sixth grade. When she got into high school in her home town of Chicago, she was already writing for community newspapers and editing a teen section. "I was always interested in journalism," she said.

Miss Washington was as determined as she was interested. She had to interrupt her journalism studies at Marquette University in Milwaukee when her husband, a serviceman, was sent to Germany. She joined him there but did not forget her goal. She became a correspondent for the *Chicago Daily Defender*, sending back stories about the lives of Army wives in Europe and other activities of service families. After she returned to Chicago, she got a staff job with the *Defender* on the basis of her dispatches and remained with the paper for four years.

One of her most memorable stories during that period was the historic civil rights march from Selma to Montgomery, Alabama. "I was down there for three weeks, and it was a beautiful experience to have as a reporter and a human being," she said. "I had never been South before and, because of my years in Germany, I had not been close to the civil rights movement until that time. The march helped me to find out which way I was going."

While on the *Defender*, Miss Washington knocked several

times on the door of the *Chicago Daily News,* one of the city's major white newspapers. "Each time," she recalled, "the editor told me I needed more preparation. I thought I had grown as much as I could, and I needed to be covering other kinds of stories."

Her break came in 1968, when, in the wake of racial rioting, the *Daily News* hired her shortly after putting L. F. Palmer, Jr., another *Defender* alumnus, on its staff. "I knew I was qualified and I was pretty sure I could do a good job, but I knew the editors would be watching me closely," Miss Washington remembered. "One editor told me he didn't expect too much of me. That was a heck of a way to start a new job."

That editor was proved wrong. Betty Washington has become a skilled and understanding reporter, covering such complex stories as Model Cities, municipal politics, race relations and public utilities. Among her accomplishments was that of convincing many people in Chicago of the importance of Model Cities, an urban renewal program.

"For a year," she said, "I had to settle for going to citizens' meetings and going through the frustrating business of not being able to get a story in unless somebody got up and screamed or cursed. But eventually the *Daily News* was running stories about this new program and what it would mean to everyone. Then other newspapers and TV picked it up. It was a very happy, rewarding feeling."

In advising black high-schoolers on their careers in journalism, Miss Washington said that working for a black or white newspaper is a "personal thing."

"You can learn a lot more on the Establishment press," she continued. "You understand how things work to a greater extent. On the black press a reporter is freer to write. You can go wild writing about slum buildings and police brutality. You won't get that kind of opportunity on white papers, especially about police brutality.

"I think it's important to be downtown, to be able to cover city hall and county board meetings. You have more access to people on the Establishment papers. And, unfortunately, you have more black readers when you're writing for the Establishment press, because the circulation of black papers is not that great."

An attractive, intense person who takes her work seriously, Miss Washington does not consider herself a reporter of only black news.

"I don't run away from stories about blacks," she explained. "When something happens that has to do with Black Panthers, I want to be there. I feel that in touchy situations like that, black reporters generally can do a better job of covering than white reporters. But I prefer to think of myself as a general assignment reporter, able to cover any kind of story."

MARILYN I. DUNCAN

The women's pages are undergoing dramatic changes on many newspapers. The emphasis is shifting from standard wedding and social stories to the reporting of more significant news, interesting features and discussion of important issues. As a result, these dailies are attracting girls who formerly spurned the women's section as too frilly and frothy. At the same time, a number of papers are, at long last, covering social news in the black community. The coverage does not match that of white social events, but gains are being made. Equally encouraging is the fact that newspapers have begun to employ black women to write about the activities of their sisters, social and otherwise.

One of these reporters is Marilyn Duncan, of the Memphis *Commercial Appeal.* Only twenty-six, she has run a gamut of assignments that a veteran journalist might envy. She has batted out profiles on such newsworthy figures as Jeannette Jennings, the first black professor at the University of Mississippi, and Mrs. Odell Horton, the president of LeMoyne-Owen College in Memphis. Her by-line has gone on a story about a black Nashville woman who runs a business school for veterans and disadvantaged youth and another about the problems of finding parents for black children available for adoption. She also did a three-part series on child abuse and a feature about black businesswomen in Memphis.

Miss Duncan is not confined to black stories, although she said she enjoys writing them. She added: "The black woman's role in journalism is an important one, especially in news about the black community. There is a tremendous amount of information here that needs to be brought out. And it has been my experience that many blacks being interviewed are more comfortable and at ease with a black reporter."

According to Miss Duncan, there are "unlimited opportunities" for black youth going into journalism.

"I would advise them," she added, "to know their field well, put all their talents to use and always tell themselves they can do better the next time than they did the last."

Miss Duncan was born in Washington, D.C., and grew up in Memphis. She attended Memphis State University before graduating from Lincoln University in Jefferson City, Missouri.

ANGELA CLAIRE PARKER

One way to a newspaper job is through an internship. A number of dailies employ college students as intern reporters during summer vacations or the regular school year. The neophyte is given general assignment duties and is watched carefully by editors, who assess him for permanent employment.

Angela Claire Parker is one of those who made the grade. In the summer of 1969, while a student at Stephens College in Columbia, Missouri, she was given an internship at the *Chicago Tribune*. She performed so well that she was named a full-time reporter the following year. Teaming up with a more experienced reporter, she helped develop and write a special series on hunger. She currently specializes in urban affairs and has covered Model Cities, housing, poverty, the courts, the zoning board of appeals and the state attorney general's fraud and complaint division.

Miss Parker, who is twenty-three years old, was born in Fort Sheridan, Illinois. During her last two years at Stephens, she took journalism courses as a special student at the University of Missouri, also in Columbia.

NANCY HICKS

Relatively few women specialize in science writing for newspapers. One of the exceptions is Nancy Hicks, by-liner of *The New York Times*. She started there in 1968 as a reporter on the Education News Desk and then became a metropolitan reporter. That same year she won the Russwurm Award of the New York Urban League, an honor given to a journalist whose work has "contributed materially to improving the plight of the unfortunate in the New York community."

In her science and medical coverage, Mrs. Hicks has reported on lead poisoning of slum children, ex-Army medics as civilian health aides, sickle-cell anemia (a disease that affects the black population almost exclusively), a black medical school and a moon walk by American astronauts. She said of her work:

"I cover general science, social science and some medicine and health. I have found it is possible to make this area meaningful to black people. Many science stories, however, are not particularly relevant to blacks, and I make no apologies for these. They are interesting and/or fun and, if done well, give me the leverage to do the stories I feel are important."

The slender young reporter has had her share of thrills in journalism. On a July morning in 1968, when she was a reporter for the *New York Post*, Mrs. Hicks was walking along Madison Avenue on her way to an assignment. Suddenly she heard the scream of sirens as two ambulances raced by her. They turned down the next cross street, and Mrs. Hicks ran toward them as they stopped a block away. She saw two policemen carrying a wounded man.

"Get down," one of the patrolmen shouted at her. "There's a sniper in the park!"

A man in a white undershirt was on the roof of a public lavatory in nearby Central Park. He had a long-barreled .45-caliber revolver with which he had killed a twenty-four-year-old woman and critically wounded an eighty-year-old man.

Instead of getting down, Nancy Hicks went into action. She bolted down the street, pounding on private doors in search of a telephone to call her paper. She finally got one, rang up her city editor and gave him the story. He then instructed her to stay with it until other reporters and photographers arrived.

There was plenty to keep her occupied until they got there. More than one hundred policemen converged on the scene as gunshots sounded through the area. Two officers, wearing bullet-proof vests, tossed tear-gas pellets onto the roof as the sniper continued firing. He was finally killed by the two policemen, who climbed ladders to the roof and shot him at close range. Mrs. Hicks had watched the action from behind a line of buses parked on Fifth Avenue. She said later in an interview for *Long Island University Magazine*:

"I had mixed feelings. As a citizen I was terrified that a man had run amok like that and shot four people. [Two officers were wounded.] As a reporter, celebrating my first anniversary in the business, I was reassured. My instinctive response to the urgency of the situation had been correct."

Nancy Hicks began "working my way into journalism" in junior high school as a reporter for its monthly newspaper. At George Washington High School in New York she was editor-in-chief of the paper, an honor that cemented her decision to major in journalism at Long Island University, where she won several honors. In her senior year, she landed a part-time job as a copygirl at the *Post* and became a reporter on that paper when she graduated.

Her advice to teen-agers weighing a news career: "Study as many different kinds of things as possible. Every young writer has to learn for himself that you don't have to write about everything you know about. Blacks understand the black story best. But the insight into human nature they have gained by understanding that story can be applied to many other subjects as well. It sometimes is good to hold the ace and play it at a later time."

JEAN PERRY

In the summer of 1966, Jean Perry was performing as a dancer in the off-Broadway production of Langston Hughes's *The Prodigal Son*. The attractive East Harlem girl had been studying modern dance on a scholarship at the Martha Graham School and planned a career in the theater. But later, at

the Fashion Institute of Technology, where she got an associate in applied arts degree, Miss Perry found that she liked
to write more than she liked to dance. She transferred to
New York University, got a journalism degree and began
looking for a job.

Her opportunity came a few weeks after graduation. At a
career conference sponsored by Theta Sigma Phi, the
women's journalism sorority, she met Christina Kirk, feature
writer for the New York *Daily News*, which has the largest
circulation of any newspaper in America. Miss Kirk thought
the young girl had promise and arranged appointments for
her with *News* editors. She was hired as an editorial trainee
after talking to four editors and submitting several samples
of her writing. Miss Perry was one of the first two black
trainees absorbed into a new program by the *News*.

Today, she is a full-fledged *News* reporter and has covered
stories about drug pushing, a policeman's funeral, fires, court
proceedings, parades, bank holdups and murders. She advises
young people seeking journalism positions to "attend all career conferences."

"At parties and panel discussions," she continued, "you'll
meet reporters who can tell you what their publication is
looking for; they are more in tune with job requirements than
most counselors and teachers. Meeting someone from a
paper is more rewarding than going into a company cold and
approaching the secretary at the entrance to the personnel
office." Miss Perry also suggested that applicants submit a
complete résumé.

Like many reporters before her, Jean Perry learned that a
newspaper office is a fast-moving, busy place where young
staffers are pretty much on their own. "Expect to train yourself," she warned. "Sometimes veteran newsmen will help you
find the lead or tell you who to call, but mostly it's your

responsibility. When you go out on a story, you may be with two or three other reporters. Sometimes you'll just be alone. When you get back to your office, you may have to call the source again because you forgot to ask a key question. But you do develop self-reliance this way. Another thing I learned was to keep reading my newspaper to see what changes the desk made in my copy. This is how a reporter begins to grow. And by just covering your assignments, you'll pick up many of the writer's tools—description, brevity and the use of active verbs."

JEANNYE THORNTON

In these turbulent times, newspapers and broadcast stations often seek opinions on issues from the "man in the street." Reporters and cameramen usually station themselves at a busy pedestrian intersection and buttonhole passers-by for their views.

Jeannye Thornton, of the *Chicago Tribune*, is one of these inquiring reporters. She asks the questions and writes the copy for "Mini 'Pinions," a *Tribune* feature. She also covers other assignments that have included the national convention of the NAACP and the Southern Christian Leadership Conference (SCLC). A native of Lynchburg, Virginia, she was graduated from Ohio State University with a B.A. in journalism.

ALMENA LOMAX

Almena Lomax, a reporter for the *San Francisco Examiner*, has packed into her more than twenty-five years of journalism a wealth of experiences. She has edited and published her own newspaper, covered civil rights marches, free-lanced for newspapers and magazines, broadcast news for a radio station and been a staffer on two white dailies. She has won the Wendell Wilkie Award for Negro Journalism and has been given other honors, including three *Examiner* citations for excellence in reporting and writing. Her appreciation of the honors is mixed with a cool, no-nonsense appraisal of her own abilities.

"I got this job [with the *Examiner*] strictly on merit," she said. "I feel I am as good as anybody in this business and better than most. Many white male reporters lack originality; they've lost heart. Around the city room they call me the reporter with a heart."

Miss Lomax put her heart into the newspaper field at an early age—seven, to be exact. When she was growing up in Chicago, an afternoon white daily, the *Evening American*, rented the basement of her house as a distributing point for neighborhood carriers. She and her brother delivered the paper from house to house. Later she sold the black *Chicago Defender* under the tracks of the old elevated railroad in the Windy City.

Her parents had been educated in Southern black colleges, and there were plenty of books around the house. She read them voraciously, along with newspapers. By the time she was ready for high school, her family had moved to Los Angeles, where her career really started. She was editor of both the school newspaper and the yearbook, taking on many writing chores as well. On her way to school each day, Almena Lomax passed the office of the *California Eagle*, a black weekly owned by Charlotta A. Bass, who was considered the dean of black journalists in Los Angeles. Mrs. Bass had purchased the paper from J. J. Neimore, founder of the *Eagle*, who was believed to have been the first black newspaperman in California.

One day Miss Lomax walked into the *Eagle* shop and asked Mrs. Bass for a job. "Can you type?" the publisher asked.

"Sure," the high school girl responded. Mrs. Bass promptly sat her down at a typewriter, gave her a big pile of community news releases and told her to go to work.

Almena Lomax had fibbed about her typing proficiency, but Mrs. Bass was so impressed by her courage and willingness to try that she let her stay on anyway. The girl learned to type by the hunt-and-peck system, getting paid $7 a week during the process.

After graduating from high school, Miss Lomax attended Los Angeles City College but gave it up after a year and a half for a full-time position on the *Eagle* at $10 a week. To augment her income, she became the first black newscaster over radio station KGFJ. She also wrote and delivered her own commercials.

Miss Lomax said that on the *Eagle* she was the first black journalist to seek out news at the likely sources—police stations, courtrooms, the coroner's office, etc. Until then, she said, black reporters were told by their editors to call a black employee of a particular city agency or department. This would not do for Almena Lomax. The petite, attractive girl marched into the police station, confronted the captain and demanded the same rights as any other reporter.

"Actually," she recounted, "they were pretty good to me after they got over the shock. Sometimes I used to get a ride home in a police car." She said she was only interested in news of the black community, "news the white papers were not printing. Nobody could sneeze without my knowing about it."

In 1943 a small black religious weekly was up for sale in Los Angeles. Scraping together the money, Miss Lomax bought it and changed its name to the *Los Angeles Tribune*.

She began by distributing free copies to the churches to acquaint the public with it. Later she altered the format, making it a paper for general news. It grew to a twenty-four-page, five-column tabloid full of lively news stories, opinion pieces and political commentary. The paper grew in importance, and so did its editor. Miss Lomax was one of the first black journalists to be accredited by the Motion Picture Academy of Arts and Sciences. Her interviews included white as well as black sources; she could get straight through by telephone to the governor of California in Sacramento, so well did he know her. At its peak, the *Tribune* reached a circulation of 25,000.

From 1960 to 1965, she made several trips to the South to report on the civil rights movement. To finance the excursions she asked *Tribune* readers to pay subscriptions in advance, and hundreds complied. When she covered the Montgomery, Alabama, march, she piled her six children into the car and headed south. She filed dispatches not only for the *Tribune* but for a number of magazines as well. She had dinner with Dr. Martin Luther King and met several other civil rights leaders, including the Reverend Ralph Abernathy.

It was Miss Lomax's first glimpse of the South. "When I saw the situation, I determined that I would *really* cover the civil rights story," she said. Eventually, she closed down her newspaper and devoted all her time to free-lancing. She joined the *San Francisco Examiner* in 1970, after a brief period as a copy editor on the *San Francisco Chronicle*.

Miss Lomax doesn't see anything inconsistent in being black and writing objectively. "I feel better equipped to be objective than white reporters," she said. "But at the same time I think I can write more humanely about human beings than most white newsmen. My point of view is human because I don't have to be a professional liberal to see human problems."

She advised black journalism students to work for black newspapers after they graduate.

"The Negro community needs journalists," she said. "Nothing is needed so badly by Negroes. Metropolitan areas, both black and white, need a good Negro press. As someone has said, it becomes a second government. The Negro press can serve as a catalytic agent; it can be a force for criticism, and it will help the Negro business community."

BARBARA CAMPBELL

Barbara Campbell is the kind of reporter who can collaborate with another reporter on a four-part series on the drug problem or write a feature on Billy Taylor, the musical director of the David Frost Show on television. She has done both and has won awards for those efforts from her newspaper, *The New York Times*. She also has covered stories on the black community, elderly people and cultural activities.

A native of Arkansas, she studied at the College of the Sequoias and was graduated from the University of California at Los Angeles. Before going to the *Times* as a news clerk in 1966, Miss Campbell had been on the staff of *Life* magazine.

6 / The Broadcast Journalists

To the outsider, television news reporting appears to be the glamorous side of journalism. The video watcher can see news being made, whether it be on the streets of New York or in the jungles of Vietnam. Then, too, the TV reporters on the air are usually handsome, well dressed and smooth-voiced. Some are celebrities whose faces are recognized everywhere and who have their own audience following.

Part of this image is true. Compared with the generally anonymous print reporter, the TV journalist is frequently in the limelight. In addition, he seems to cover more exciting stories—riots, shootings, political confrontations, etc. This impression comes largely from the fact that television journalism tends to concentrate on news that lends itself to pictures, such as fires, unruly crowds, beauty pageants and the like.

Although TV reporting has more surface glamour, the techniques of gathering and presenting the news are similar to those used by newspapermen. Reporters must go to the news sources, conduct interviews and, in many cases, write stories for broadcast. The men and women who read news on the air may or may not write their own copy. In any radio or television news operation there are a number of rewrite men who are never seen on camera.

Blacks are no longer a novelty in TV journalism. They are represented on the three major networks—CBS, ABC and NBC—as well as on a number of radio and television stations

97

throughout the country. Their ranks are not as large as they should be, but they're growing. Here are some of these electronic journalists:

HAL WALKER

Washington is the beat of Hal Walker, a CBS news correspondent who has covered a number of major events in his television career. He also has worked on several special reports, including the seven-part "Black America" series and "A Dialogue With Whitey," for which he won a special "Emmy" and other awards. His straight news reporting has ranged from campus riots to Capitol Hill debates. Walker frequently appears on the CBS Evening News with Walter Cronkite.

Hal Walker was born thirty-eight years ago in Darlington, South Carolina, and was reared in New York City. He graduated from Denison University in Ohio, later taking postgraduate work at Syracuse University and the State University of New York. He was in the Army from 1954 through January, 1958. His first writing job after his discharge was with the New York State Department of Mental Hygiene. In 1963 he broke into television with WTOP-TV News in Washington, covering the White House, the State Department and other national news sources.

GIL NOBLE

In 1957 Harlem radio station WLIB hired Gil Noble as an $80-a-week announcer. To make ends meet, the young man moonlighted as a clerk in a bank. He used any spare time to pursue his first interest—playing jazz piano, which he had taught himself since childhood.

Currently he is one of television's outstanding newsmen, anchoring his own twice-weekly fifteen-minute newscast and hosting an hour-long weekly series over WABC-TV in New York. When he has time, he still plays jazz on the baby grand piano he bought in 1954 after his discharge from the Army.

Gil Noble is more than a studio news announcer. He doubles as an on-the-street reporter for WABC-TV's evening "Eyewitness News" report, covering spot stories in the city. "Like It Is," his weekly show, focuses on life in the black community and has garnered a number of award nominations and wide praise for its hard-hitting quality.

Noble's TV career actually began in Russia. In 1959 he and Norma Jean Johnson, a New York nurse, were picked by the State Department as black models for an American cultural and industrial exhibition in Moscow (the scene of Richard Nixon's famous "Kitchen Debate" with Premier Nikita Khrushchev). The couple's trade fair stint blossomed into a romance, and they decided to get married. When news of the engagement got around, the many American newsmen and publicists covering the exhibit were delighted. They had been desperately searching for fresh stories about the fair, and this seemed made to order. The journalists arranged with the then United States ambassador, Llewellyn Thompson, to have the "models" married in a Moscow civil court, with the ceremony being followed by a lavish caviar and champagne reception at the ambassador's mansion. Noble became popular with the television correspondents, who helped him decide to switch to video journalism.

But it wasn't until 1967 that Gil Noble was able to carry out this resolve. The Newark riots broke out that year as he was trying out for a reporter's job at WABC's Channel 7 news. He handled a riot assignment so competently that he was quickly given a permanent position. Two years later he won the John B. Russwurm Award for reporting that improved the plight of New York City minority groups. He was cited for "sustained excellence in interpreting, analyzing and reporting of the news." Noble has interviewed a number of prominent persons, including the late Robert F. Kennedy, Mrs. Martin Luther King and Muhammad Ali.

Noble takes his work seriously. He also is concerned about the role of blacks in the media, feeling that they are not at all well enough represented. He told an interviewer for the magazine *Still Here*: "Maybe one tenth of one percent of the stations have made one tenth of one percent of an improvement in hiring blacks."

On the question of objectivity in journalism, Noble said that the only way a black reporter can be objective is "to tell it like it is.

"A black newsman is mandated to take a cold, hard look at his profession, which is built on the foundation of objectivity, of telling the truth," Noble continued. "He must realize, however, that this foundation is false when it comes to telling the story of black people."

Noble also feels there is a crying need for black news directors and editors. "And black people shouldn't stop at that point," he continued. "They should own radio and television stations."

He offered this advice to black youngsters thinking of media careers: "Try to become as proficient in your skills as possible. Chart a course that is similar to mine, but do not stay at my level. When you've become established, go back to the black community. Try to create black-owned radio and TV stations. Blacks should start their own lines of communication for channeling information into the black community."

Gil Noble was one of two sons born to a Harlem gas station

owner and a mother who taught in a community center. He
began to teach himself piano in elementary school, with a
music career as his goal. By the time he had finished junior
high school, he was disenchanted with ghetto education.
"Like a lot of Negro kids," he said, "I lied about my address
so I could go to DeWitt Clinton High School in the Bronx."

After graduating from DeWitt Clinton, he enrolled as a
night student at City College, working days in the stacks of
the New York Public Library. The draft interrupted his studies in 1952, and he was sent to Virginia as an Army medic.
Discharged two years later, he returned to New York, took
a clerical job, rented an apartment and did part-time modeling, piano playing and occasional "voice-overs" for radio
commercials. When he moved to WLIB, he had to take a $55
cut in salary from his clerk's job.

EDITH HUGGINS

As a teen-ager in St. Joseph, Missouri, Edith Huggins prepared for a broadcasting career by being a disc jockey on a
local radio station. But the break that was to make her one
of the country's top TV news reporters came after a series of
occupations ranging from nursing to acting in major television dramas. Today she has her own morning news show
over WCAU-TV in Philadelphia and is on again at 6 P.M.
as a member of the "Big News" team on Channel 10. She
researches, writes and broadcasts her own stories, many of
which stress the human interest side of the news. But she is
just as much at home reporting on fashion trends as on a city
council session.

Following her disc jockey days, Edith Huggins matricu-
lated as a music major at the University of Nebraska, where
she appeared on a number of educational television pro-

grams. Switching to nursing, she graduated cum laude from the State University of New York and began work in that field. It was while she was on the staff of a New York City hospital that she was able to resume her acting. She got a part in NBC's "The Doctors" and doubled as a technical consultant for the series. Her looks, voice and talent brought her to the attention of WCAU, a CBS affiliate, which put her on the news staff in 1966. Mrs. Huggins hasn't completely given up acting. Recently she has appeared in video episodes of "The Doctors," "Love of Life" and "The Edge of Night."

But journalism is her primary love. A dedicated, conscientious reporter, she is pursuing a master's degree in communications at Temple University. Mrs. Huggins also has some firm ideas on the use of blacks in electronic journalism.

"Despite the number of blacks involved in radio and television, the media still reeks of tokenism and of hiring to fulfill Federal Communications Commission regulations," she asserted. "Because race has been in the background for so many years in the media, persons in managerial and executive positions are a rare breed. The argument is obvious: If there has been limited time or exposure in an industry, who then can reach executive or managerial heights? The answer: stations must be forced to hire and forced to train. Those black people already in the media must seek and prepare for more responsible jobs. Others, in turn, must come along to increase the black ranks and begin the upward progression. Because television news reaches more people than any other source, blacks must have a greater part in the selection, reporting and producing of what is seen and heard on the air."

Mrs. Huggins also advised blacks to train for the new fields in television, particularly cable TV and video cassettes.

"Soon," she said, "these forms of information will give viewers a chance to select only what they want to see. Because of this increased selectivity, there must be blacks involved in all of these new areas to avoid any blocking out of the black message. It's these new horizons that minority groups must consider, must train for and must demand be opened."

JIM GIGGANS

Being a war correspondent is a tough, dangerous job. Most of the American reporters in Southeast Asia are young, vigorous and experienced. They have to be. To report a war, the combat correspondent often must travel to the scene of the action. He hears the bullets whine and sees men die. Through it all, he must keep a cool head so that he can write or broadcast what he has seen.

The Vietnam conflict is the first war to have been brought into the living rooms of this nation. Battle scenes frequently have been shown on television, with the TV reporter describing the action.

One of these newsmen is Jim Giggans, an ABC correspondent, who has reported from South Vietnam, Cambodia and Laos. He made the jump from network news trainee to war correspondent in only two years.

That isn't the only surprising thing about Giggans's present role. He is an accomplished pianist and has sung in operas. As a news trainee, he wrote and directed several programs in the "Directions" series of religious documentaries.

Giggans was born in Bremerton, Washington, and is a graduate of the University of Washington at Seattle. He also holds a graduate degree from the Sorbonne in Paris, where he studied from 1966 to 1968. Before joining the ABC-TV network, he was assistant manager of public relations for

Airco and a member of the P.R. staff of the Mobil Oil Corporation.

JOHN JOHNSON, JR.

Few blacks have attained managerial or executive spots in the news media. One of them is John Johnson, Jr., a producer-director for ABC news, who is employed primarily in specials and documentaries.

A former associate professor of fine arts at Lincoln University in Pennsylvania, Johnson also has lectured on urban affairs, the problems of decentralization in education and ghetto youth. He joined ABC in 1968, becoming associate producer of "Three Young Americans in Search of Survival," a two-hour special on environment that won wide critical acclaim. The next year he wrote and produced "The Welfare Game," an hour-long examination of the failures and successes of public assistance programs in the United States. In 1970 Johnson was associate producer and director of the first program in ABC News's three-part series on ecology, "Mission Possible: They Care for a City." He also directed Part 1 of the ABC News special "To All the World's Children" in November, 1970.

Johnson recollected that his first producing assignment for ABC-TV almost destroyed his desire to work in the television industry. In the summer of 1969, the network was presenting a series called "Time for Americans," which dealt with minorities and the issues causing conflict in the nation. Assigned as the producer of a series show on welfare, Johnson, after weeks of research, assembled a panel of two senators, a spokesman for the Welfare Rights Organization, a welfare recipient and a university professor to discuss the policies and future of welfare in this country.

"At the conclusion of the taping, I was satisfied that the program would bring new insight into the problems of welfare and also point up the raging conflicts involved in the issue," Johnson said.

The tapes were held in the ABC library in New York until air time. Meanwhile, Johnson had to leave for Washington and Chicago on another story. When he returned to New York a few days later, he called for the tapes so he could edit them down to the allocated air time. He was informed that both prints—one for airing and one for protection—were missing. Later that day Johnson learned that the tapes had been destroyed.

"Both tapes had been erased, and a sporting event had been taped over my show," Johnson said. "At this point, my first thoughts were naturally of sabotage. I felt that someone had destroyed the show because they didn't want any black producer at ABC. The likelihood of erasing a show is so remote that it is easy to arrive at conclusions of foul play."

An investigation, however, disclosed that the loss was an accident caused by summer replacement help. A supervisor connected with the incident was fired, Johnson said.

"I did the show again," Johnson continued. "It went on the air unnoticed, and perhaps for good reason. The feeling engendered in the original show was lost, and the second tape was just not as good as the first.

"The incident, though, was a kind of catalytic experience for me. I have been determined ever since to make it in a tough industry—an industry that needs more blacks in the behind-the-scenes creative and policy-making levels."

Johnson recommended that black college students major in journalism and film if they want a career in broadcast journalism. He added:

"We are about to enter an era where television program-

ming will be challenged by the advent of cassettes and cable
TV. Now is the time to prepare for entrance into a medium
whose full potential has not been reached. The informational,
educational boom is here, and it is important that blacks have
a hand in the formation and direction of a medium that can
mold men's minds."

A native New Yorker, Johnson graduated from that city's
High School of Art and Design and received his bachelor's
and master's degrees from the City University of New York.
Before teaching at Lincoln, he was an assistant principal,
dean of students and faculty and chairman of the arts department of an inner city school in New York City.

Despite his crammed schedule, Johnson finds time for his
two favorite avocations, painting and sculpting. He has had
several one-man showings of his work and was one of six
black painters chosen to participate in New York's Metropolitan Museum of Art exhibition "Harlem on My Mind" in
1969. He also has written about African art.

BARBARA J. CAFFIE

If a movie producer were looking for a story of a poor girl
who makes good in big-city television, he would find the
ideal source in Barbara J. Caffie, news reporter for WJW-TV
in Cleveland. Mrs. Caffie, the mother of three children, was
a dime-store sales clerk, nurse's aide, typist and secretary
before she got into television in 1969 at the age of thirty-
three. "I know what it means to be short of food, to be without lights and gas and not be able to go to the doctor," she
said.

Mrs. Caffie came to Cleveland as a bride in 1956 from
Wooster, Ohio, where she went to high school and was active

in singing groups. After a series of jobs, she was hired as a
secretary at WJW when a white girl reporter left.

"I had three things going for me," Mrs. Caffie recalled.
"There was a news slot open, the station was seeking a black
girl reporter and I had what my husband has described as
a 'gift of gab.'"

Barbara Caffie had three auditions for the spot. The first
one was a flop, the second was a little better and the third
convinced the news editor that she had potential for on-cam-
era reporting.

"He was white, and I'll always be grateful for the help
and encouragement he gave me," she said. "This was a new
thing for me. I was setting my eyes on the stars and was
going to reach them. Previously, I had lived every day as it
came. Then, all of a sudden, I was part of a black awareness.
I had always thought that I had been denied certain jobs
because of my color. But the station was looking for a black
woman. I felt I could do the work, remain black and mingle
on both sides of the fence. I don't feel we should be hung up
on the fact of being black."

Mrs. Caffie works a nine-to-five day and sometimes longer
when a hot, breaking story keeps her on overtime. She still
finds time to do her own housework, cooking and sewing.
"I'm a full-time newswoman, but I also try to be a full-time
mother," she explained. "I also try to be a part of the community by making guest speeches and appearances at various
functions."

She said she loves her job, frustrations and all. "When I
cover a fire, I know that my face will get dirty and my stock-
ings will run. But that's part of the news business. I've learned
to cut and edit my own film. I've learned, too, that it's not the
reporter who is the most important person in the interview.

It's the person being interviewed. He is the real basis for the encounter."

One of the frustrations Mrs. Caffie encountered was the same as that experienced by other black reporters covering stories with white camera and sound crews. "It used to make me really angry when news sources would address my cameraman and ignore me," she said. "But I got over that. I realized that the persons would eventually have to come to me. I was the reporter, and I was in charge. The technical crew is responsible to me. This gave me a feeling of importance and strength."

Mrs. Caffie feels that much more should be done to bring blacks into the news media. "I'm not satisfied with what's been done," she declared. "They owe this to me. I had help, but I had the qualifications for the job. There are qualified blacks in all walks of life who can do as well as the white man, or better."

In advising black youth on a career in her field, Mrs. Caffie said: "You've got to be better than a white man or woman. If you're a black woman, television is wide open. But don't be hotheaded or domineering. You can accomplish much more by being gracious and showing respect for all people."

She also stressed the need for education, pointing out that her lack of college and journalism training proved to be a handicap when she was getting started. "Even now," she went on, "I read every newspaper, magazine and book I can. When I come across something important, I type it out so I will remember it."

Mrs. Caffie had one further piece of advice for black youngsters entertaining ideas of a journalism career.

"Do what you must on your own," she said. "Don't expect other people to open doors for you. When you do become successful, it will mean much more to you if you've done it

yourself. And don't let racists and bigots discourage you. In
our field, there is no color. I work with thirteen white men,
and they treat me as a woman—not a black woman, but a
woman.

"So I say to everyone—black, white, green or purple: If you
think you can do this job, try it. It's a great way to enjoy
life while making a good living."

WILLIAM C. MATNEY, JR.

One of the most frequently seen faces in television is that of
William Matney, Jr., NBC News White House correspondent
in Washington. In addition to appearing on regular network
newscasts, he also has been on the "Today" show and numerous other broadcasts. His varied career has included coverage of the Presidential conventions of 1964 and 1968, President Nixon's 1970 European trip, critical labor negotiations
between the United Auto Workers and the "Big Three" of
the automotive industry and the Gemini space flights. He
has served as a correspondent on several NBC "White Paper"
specials and documentaries.

It can truly be said that Bill Matney came up through the
ranks. He was born in Bluefield, West Virginia, on the campus of Bluefield State Teachers College, where his father
taught economics and business administration and his
mother, music. The family subsequently moved to Detroit,
where he finished his elementary and high school training.

Matney's college education at Wayne State University in
Detroit was interrupted after his sophomore year when he
went into the Army Air Corps during World War II. After
his discharge he enrolled at the University of Michigan, where
he earned his B.A. degree and was a letterman on the track
team.

His first journalism job came in 1946 as sports editor of the *Michigan Chronicle*, a black weekly in Detroit. He remained there for fifteen years, becoming successively sports editor, city editor and managing editor for the last ten years. Under his guidance, the *Chronicle* went from a ten-page weekly of 17,000 circulation to a thirty-six-page paper of 50,000 circulation and one of the top black newspapers in the country.

In 1961 Bill Matney joined the *Detroit News*, one of the city's major dailies, as a staff reporter. He later became senior rewrite man, feature writer and assistant to the city editor. He moved to NBC News in Chicago in 1963, and three years later he was named network correspondent for the Midwest with a seventeen-state responsibility. He had his own ten-minute newscast on both television and radio.

His television honors have included the International Pioneer Club's "Man of the Year," Sigma Delta Chi's "outstanding performance" citation, the Capitol Press Club's national award for broadcast journalism and an "Emmy" from the National Academy of Television Arts and Sciences for 1967–68.

CAROL JENKINS

At one time Carol Jenkins thought she had her life all mapped out. She got a bachelor's degree in speech pathology at Boston University and then a master's in the same subject at New York University. She was fully qualified for a career as a speech pathologist.

"But then I decided this wasn't me," the vivacious black woman recalled. What *was* her, it turned out, was journalism, which she enthusiastically practices over WOR-TV, Channel 9, in New York City. She and her crew cover an average of six stories before noon. She also does a daily one-hour show called "Straight Talk" on race and other issues.

But she likes her work most when she is out after the news, competing with other TV stations in the metropolitan area. Channel 9 is the smallest of the video news operations in New York, but that doesn't stop Carol Jenkins from being one of the toughest competitors in the business. Once, New York Governor Nelson Rockefeller pulled up in his limousine to a building where he was to make a speech. He had sent word that there would be no interviews beforehand.

As a crowd milled around his car, Miss Jenkins stepped forward and greeted the Governor. Assuming that she was just another voter, Rockefeller smilingly offered his hand. She shook it, but with her other hand she grabbed the microphone being held by her engineer. In a twinkling, the startled Governor found himself staring into the mike, with Miss Jenkins shooting questions at him.

On another story—the Newark, New Jersey, teachers' strike —the comely newswoman got an exclusive interview with the strike leader while other reporters were looking vainly for her. Miss Jenkins simply used common sense to find the union leader's name in the telephone book. When she called there was no answer, but Miss Jenkins had a nagging suspicion that she was on the right track. She had one of her crewmen drive her to the woman's house, where she pounded on the door for several minutes. Eventually the sleepy-eyed teachers' leader let her in. Miss Jenkins got the interview over a hot cup of coffee. When it was all over, the union boss revealed that the only reason she had admitted Miss Jenkins was because she had thought she was a neighbor.

"You have to have three things to endure the incredible pace and competition," Miss Jenkins said—"a sense of humor, love of news work and love of yourself. The humorous element shows us that, despite all the gloom and doom, we're still here."

But achieving her goal was serious business, and she did it the hard way. For several months she conducted a fifteen-minute interview program on a small New Jersey station at three in the morning. "The transmitter was so weak that you had to shake your radio to hear it," she laughed.

From there she went to radio station WNYC in New York, where she wrote, produced and delivered her own show in a project sponsored by the Full Opportunities Commission of the National Academy of Television Arts and Sciences.

But it was as secretary at CBS in New York that she got her chance at the Channel 9 spot. In the position she met television people with information about available jobs. One tip led to an interview and being hired at WOR. "Don't belittle any secretarial or clerical job in the TV industry," she advised young aspirants for television news. "So much seems to be a case of being in the right place at the right time."

This is the right time for the twenty-six-year-old TV star, but she's not always sure she's in the right place. She finds that being a black reporter puts her in a difficult position. "I know there are some black people who think I'm a sell-out. In some ways, I am."

She told of the time when her station wanted her to cover a fancy reception at the Waldorf-Astoria Hotel, although she really wanted to report on a new school opening in Harlem. Her superiors won the argument, and she went to the hotel. But she hasn't lost all of the disputes by any means. As she gained in experience and stature, her judgment became more and more respected. Now she is able to cover a number of black stories simply by convincing her boss that they are newsworthy.

Ernest Johnston, Jr., *New York Post* reporter.

William J. Drummond, *Los Angeles Times* reporter.
Photo courtesy Bill Varie, L. A. Times

L. F. "Lu" Palmer, *Chicago Daily News* reporter.

Jeannye Thornton, *Chicago Tribune* reporter.

Ovie Carter, *Chicago Tribune* photographer.
Photo courtesy
Chicago Tribune

Rodney Whitaker, Memphis *Commercial Appeal*.
Photo courtesy Bob Williams,
The Commercial Appeal

Marilyn Duncan, Memphis *Commercial Appeal*.
Photo courtesy Bob Williams,
The Commercial Appeal

Nancy Hicks, *The New York Times*.

William J. Raspberry, *Washington Post* columnist.

Thomas A. Johnson, reporter, *The New York Times*.
Photo courtesy The New York Times

Henri E. Wittenberg, reporter, *The Detroit News.*

George Hardin, Memphis *Commercial Appeal.*

Austin Scott, Associated Press.

John L. Taylor, United Press International.
Photo courtesy UPI

Melba Tolliver, WABC-TV, New York.

Edith Huggins, WCAU-TV, Philadelphia.

Valerie Coleman (far right), KRON-TV, San Francisco.

Barbara J. Caffie, WJU-TV, Cleveland.

Bill Matney, NBC News correspondent.

Chris Borgen, WCBS-TV News
correspondent.

Don Phelps, KOMO Radio &
TV, Seattle.
Photo courtesy Camera-Craft

Charlayne Hunter, *The New
York Times.*
Photo courtesy Tim Kantor

Hal Walker, CBS News correspondent.
Photo courtesy CBS News

Gil Noble, WABC-TV Eyewitness
News correspondent.
*Photo courtesy Wagner
International Photos*

John Dotson, *Newsweek* Los Angeles Bureau Chief.

Audreen Ballard, *Redbook* editor.

Photo courtesy Redbook *magazine*

Lerone Bennett, Jr., Senior Editor, *Ebony* magazine.

Ruth N. Ross, *Newsweek.*

Photo courtesy Bernard Gotfryd, Newsweek

Hans J. Massaquoi, Managing Editor, and Herbert Nipson, Executive Editor, *Ebony* magazine.

Photo courtesy Hal A. Franklin, II, Ebony—Jet—Tan

Ernest Dunbar, former Senior Editor, *Look* magazine.
Photo courtesy Look

Frank M. Seymour.

Vince Cullers, Vince Cullers
Advertising.
Photo courtesy Black Enterprise

Roy Eaton, Vice President and
Music Director, Benton & Bowles,
Inc.

Douglass Alligood, RCA.

Junius Edwards, Junius Edwards, Inc.
Photo courtesy Black Enterprise

Howard Sanders, Howard Sanders
Advertising.
Photo courtesy Black Enterprise

Joan Murray, Zebra Associates.
Photo courtesy
Black Enterprise

Harry A. Robinson, Director of Public Relations, National Conference of Christians and Jews, with his secretary, Mrs. Verbina Bain.
Photo courtesy Camera Arts Studio

Her "Straight Talk" show also is a demanding responsibility. She takes on controversial issues and must be strictly
impartial when opposing guests are verbally hammering away
at each other. When she aired the Vietnam war controversy,
she was accused in letters of being on the side of the antiwar
speakers. "I was leaning over backward being nice to both
sides," she said. "Maybe it was the Afro hair style I wore
that day that made some persons think I was partial."

Carol Jenkins was born in Alabama but grew up in New
York in a comfortable, middle-class home. Her parents own
and operate a printing trades school at which she once
worked, with the title of vice president. She hopes the future
will see the emergence of black management in broadcasting
as a means of more black expression in the medium.

CHRIS BORGEN

Every now and then a newsman is caught up in the event he
is covering. He is placed in a position where he has to leave
his role as an observer to take part in the action. No one
knows this more than Chris Borgen, a reporter for WCBS-TV
News in New York.

In October of 1970, Borgen, an experienced reporter, was
assigned to cover a series of violent outbreaks at New York
City prisons. At the Queens jail, prisoners had seized five
guards hostage as a means of enforcing their demands for
better conditions. At one point a dispute arose between the
convicts and prison authorities over how many hostages
would be released if the city, as the prisoners insisted, set up
a special court to set bail for a number of inmates.

The prisoners issued a notice that they would talk only to
Borgen. The thirty-eight-year-old reporter agreed to meet
six inmates in the jail's visiting room. After discussing the

issue with the newsman for several minutes, one prisoner asked him: "What should we do?"

"I can't tell you," Borgen replied. "I'm not here to tell you what to do. I can only tell you what my understanding of the situation is." He explained that he was under the impression that the convicts had promised to free two of the hostages when the court met and the other three afterward.

The tension in the visitors' room rose. "Do you mean we have to release the two hostages?" the inmate persisted.

Borgen held his ground until one of the negotiators sighed and said: "Well, I guess we'll have to let two of them go." The two guards were released to Borgen, who then headed back to his office to broadcast his story.

The following day, Borgen, in an interview with *Newsday*, revealed how he had agonized over the situation. "I wanted to cry out, 'Yes, for God's sake release them,'" he said. But he didn't, he added, because this would have meant losing his objectivity as a reporter.

"More and more, the media are playing a role," he noted. "Sometimes it's being used by people, and somewhere along the line we'll have to make a decision on whether we'll allow ourselves to be used."

Chris Borgen, a native of New York, has been working for WCBS-TV since 1966 and was named correspondent in 1969 after distinguishing himself by his coverage of the Newark racial riots and a neighborhood school crisis. During the prison riot he made exclusive live behind-the-walls reports from the "Tombs" house of detention. He also has served as the anchorman on the Channel 2 Sunday news programs, the "Mid-Day Report," "Eye on New York" and "The Sunday Report."

Borgen attended the City University of New York and Columbia University. Before going to WCBS-TV, he was the moderator of a television series, "Experts Answer," sponsored by the United States Information Agency for broadcast in Europe, Asia, Africa and Latin America. Previously he had covered the Algerian war for French television and the NBC radio network.

MELBA TOLLIVER

Channel 7's "Eyewitness News" broadcast in New York has zoomed to popularity in recent years because of its lively, informal and sometimes irreverent handling of the news. One reason for the success of this news team lies in a pert, winsome former nurse named Melba Tolliver. Her warm manner and infectious grin have won her thousands of fans who also applaud her for incisive, compassionate reporting. Witnessing a shooting on Broadway, she tended the victim, called an ambulance and then summoned a camera crew to the scene, where she broadcast a dramatic eyewitness story.

Miss Tolliver's entrance into television has a touch of Horatio Alger. Dissatisfied with nursing, she went to work for ABC in 1967 as a secretary in the news department. "I was trying then to get into television," she said. "I had done a little modeling, but this job offered me my first real chance at TV."

Her break came when the American Federation of Television and Radio Artists struck the network. Miss Tolliver, along with other office employees, was pressed into service as an announcer. With just one day's warning she was on the air with a program called "News With the Woman's Touch." The strike ended two weeks later, but the management of WABC-TV was so pleased with her efforts that they made her a news trainee. A few months later there was another strike, and she was again given on-the-air duties. The company also sent her to Columbia and New York universities for additional journalism training. At New York University she quickly rose to the head of a newswriting class, and by the end of the semester she was turning out professional copy. In 1968 WABC-TV elevated Miss Tolliver to full-time reporter.

As the only girl on "Eyewitness News," Melba Tolliver has the entire New York metropolitan area as her beat. She is frequently on the streets with a camera crew, covering everything from bank holdups to housing demonstrations. Off-beat feature stories are included in her assignments. She has no trouble keeping up with her colleagues professionally, but she does envy their need for only minimum grooming before going before the TV camera.

"When the men come back from a story, they can just comb their hair and go on," she explained. "When I come back, my hair is often a mess, especially if I've been at a fire or something. And the viewers do notice if my hair looks a little different."

Miss Tolliver was born in Rome, Georgia, and grew up in Akron, Ohio. In high school she excelled in history and current events and played violin in the orchestra. After getting her diploma, she went to New York to study at the Bellevue School of Nursing, graduating with honors. While a "scrub" nurse at Bellevue Hospital she began thinking of a different career. She enrolled at the American Academy of Dramatic Arts to study speech, acting and theater arts. This led to modeling and TV acting assignments, including parts in "A Man Called Adam," "Seconds" and "Coronet Blue."

In 1970 Melba Tolliver received the New York Urban League's Russwurm Award for her news broadcasting.

In an interview, Miss Tolliver was asked how it is to be a black reporter on television.

"Being black and being a reporter is no different, really, than being black and being anything else in this society," she replied.

You learn very quickly that, in addition to your expected professional role, you almost always have to perform a number of auxiliary roles—because you're black —and in my case because I'm black and female.

My primary role, as I see it, is the same as that of any other reporter: to gather and organize facts and information that constitute a news story—and to communicate the story within the requirements and limitations of television. My auxiliary roles, on the other hand, are more difficult to define because they shift and change according to the temper of the times and the needs of others. Most of the people I work with—assignment editors, producers, news directors, station vice-presidents and public relations personnel—seem to have very little real knowledge or understanding of black people. For the most part, they have had almost no personal, ongoing contact with blacks. And until the mid-1960s, when the major news agencies began to actively recruit blacks, most of them had probably never worked with blacks on a day-to-day basis, despite the fact that for years they had been making decisions that affected the lives of great numbers of blacks.

As a result, she continued, she often finds herself taking on the role of educator—a role that blacks have traditionally assumed whenever they've been among the first to enter fields that were previously all white. Miss Tolliver said that her educational work consists of pointing out and constructively criticizing discriminatory practices and patterns on news media that result in poor and inadequate coverage of blacks.

"The role of educator means refusing to operate under the double standard often imposed on black reporters," she explained. "It means not accepting the doublethink of an assignment editor who takes it upon himself to decide 'there might be trouble' if he sent me out to Newark's white North Ward—or black Central Ward—with a white crew. It means talking with that editor until I've convinced him that what he's doing simply reinforces the racism that we are supposed to oppose. The role also means discouraging editors, producers and others from assigning me to a certain story because I'm black or because I'm a woman and someone thinks the story needs a 'feminine touch'—or keeping me off a story because I'm black or because I'm a woman and the assignment is a 'man's story.' It means using every opportunity to encourage assignment editors and producers to see me as a reporter who, in addition to being black and female, is a lot of other things—a total human being whose professional development ought not to be restricted because of my race or sex."

Miss Tolliver also believes that her educational responsibilities extend to the community as well. She feels she has an obligation to share with other black people the knowledge she has gained about television news as a means of helping them understand the strengths and weaknesses of the medium. She added:

The black reporter, in addition to being an educator, is also a symbol. This is especially true in TV, where a black reporter on camera is as much the message as is the news story he is there to communicate. In effect, the black reporter, simply by his presence on the screen, conveys a message to an audience of millions—telling

them, without words, something about his company, its
hiring practices, its attitude about race relations. For
the blacks in the audience, the black reporter symbol-
izes the inroads they have made in an industry that until
a few years ago did very little to acknowledge their
existence, much less encourage their participation.

Educators, symbols and image makers are just a few
of the roles that black reporters must assume in this society. There are many more. And until we reach the
point in this country—and in the communications industry—where people are more concerned about issues and
performance than they are about race and sexual iden-
tity, I'm afraid that black reporters—both men and
women—will continue to have not one but several roles
and will never be considered "just another reporter,"
expected to perform the same role as any other reporter.

Melba Tolliver advised young persons seeking a television
news career to write for appointments with people in the
field. "Ask them what it's like and how they got started. Ask
them how things have changed since they began and how
these changes will affect your preparation for the same career."

She also suggested that high school and college students
try to get a news job during summer vacations to find out
what journalism is really like. And she recommended working
for school newspapers. "If your school doesn't have a paper,
help start one," she said.

"Fortunately," Miss Tolliver stated, "journalism is one
career that doesn't require a lot of complicated or expensive
tools to practice. You can begin to exercise and sharpen your
skills anytime, anywhere, by simply being interested in what's
happening around you—observing, listening, asking ques-

tions, reading newspapers and magazines, listening to news programs, watching films and documentaries and checking them all for style as well as content. And you need only a pencil, paper and discipline to begin writing your own stories."

She urged students not to wait until they have finished high school before checking into college journalism programs. Each request for an application should be accompanied by a request for scholarship information, she said.

VALERIE D. COLEMAN

Valerie Coleman, former beauty queen, Air Force "brat" and world traveler, is one of the busiest girls in television. As a full-time staffer for KRON-TV in San Francisco, she produces and is host of a series called "Target," a discussion program focusing on the problems of the core city and urban communities. She also is a reporter and co-anchor of an evening show called "Newswatch Saturday Supplement," which offers local feature stories and pays special attention to the needs and activities of minority communities.

She started at KRON in 1969 as a special reports researcher after receiving her master's degree in journalism from Columbia University. As an undergraduate, she had majored in journalism at San Jose State College in California, working for both the campus television and radio stations.

"This exposure," she related, "was invaluable in preparing me for journalism as I know it today."

It was while she was at San Jose State that Valerie Dickerson (her name before her marriage) was elected 1968 National College Queen, the first black girl to win the honor. Her journalism training came in handy in her frequent inter-

views with the press and in recording her impressions of
her reign over the campus radio and television stations.

"During this time," she said, "I decided that it was im-
perative that more blacks become actively involved in television. I am greatly concerned over the misconceptions
about black people and the movement. It was this motiva-
tion that played a great part in my decision to enter news
programming as opposed to entertainment."

Mrs. Coleman feels that she has a special mission to accomplish in television, in addition to being a good reporter.
She said:

Unfortunately, TV has a bad history in the minds of
minority communities. There was little consideration
used in the approach and techniques employed by television when reporting the events of the black community. The result is that it's a hard job to be a black
reporter. One must first break down the misconceptions
to pave the way for the trust and openness that's vital
to a reporter.

I have found that while it's fashionable to call for
more minority reporters, producers and directors, it's
not so fashionable for the one who holds such a position.
You are held responsible for mistakes made by television. Your commitment to the community from which
you came is questioned.

I'm working to change this image. I believe the
reason for it is the black community's lack of sophistica-
tion in how to use television and the other media. They
have been letting the media use them. Young blacks
should seriously consider television journalism as the
only way we can inform blacks of the power they
possess.

Most of Mrs. Coleman's childhood years were spent in foreign countries. Her father was a lieutenant colonel in the Air Force and had frequent changes of assignment. Part of her early education was in Kent, England, and Tokyo, Japan, where she remained until her first year of high school. She then entered college in Great Falls, Montana, where her father was stationed for five years, his longest tour of duty in one place. She transferred to San Jose State when her father retired and the family moved to Riverside, California.

Married in 1971, Valerie Coleman feels that television is an ideal job for mixing career and marriage. "Plus which," she said, "once a woman is established in television, the opportunities for free-lance work are phenomenal. There aren't as many openings for women in TV as there should be, but once you've made it, it's really great."

DON G. PHELPS

Don Phelps, a big-framed man who broadcasts news and commentary over KOMO television and radio in Seattle, is considered controversial because he offers his own views of touchy issues. This is all right with Phelps. If some individual or organization resents what he says about them, he offers them equal time on the air. The Seattle Police Department got equal time when Phelps accused certain officers of brutality.

To some blacks, Phelps is considered an "Uncle Tom." To numerous whites, he's a radical. "Many people are afraid to express their opinions," he said. "I'm glad to do it. I speak for myself." He explained that he does not profess to represent any minority or group. On certain broadcasts he deals with a minority problem or approach. On others, race is not a part of his commentary. He appears on TV twice a week as part of a ninety-minute news program. On radio, he has five-minute commentaries three days a week and the tapes are repeated three other days. He is free to pick any subject, and his range includes the entire city. He usually checks out his own stories and gets other ideas from local and out-of-town newspapers. When he chooses a black story, it's because he feels it's of general interest. "Anything good for black people is good for white people," he said.

All this has made Don Phelps a prominent man in Seattle. People stop him on the street and offer opinions on his last broadcast. Frequently, the KOMO switchboard lights up after a particular program as listeners call in to express anger or agreement with Phelps's position. When he first appeared on television two years ago, the station got mail telling it to "get that nigger off the air." Now, Phelps says, most of the opposing letters and calls attack his views without mentioning race. However, he still gets hate mail, he added.

In his freewheeling broadcasts, the forty-two-year-old Phelps has swung verbal punches at local personalities, labor unions and companies that cause oil slicks in the harbor. His radio program is called "Black Seattle, the Central Area," where most blacks live in the city.

Phelps's commentaries are often triggered by breaking news stories. One example was a front-page newspaper story about the fact that Seattle police were using undercover agents in the public schools as a means of fighting drug abuse. After reading the article, Phelps conferred with KOMO staff reporters and photographers who were familiar with the situation. He then checked with police and school officials, anti-drug organizations and others. From his findings he whipped together a commentary that supported the police chief and the mayor in the undercover move. As usual with a Don Phelps broadcast, there were pro and con reactions from his audience.

Phelps got into journalism in a roundabout way. When he graduated from high school, he got a scholarship to the Cornish School of Allied Arts in Seattle, where he studied voice for three years. (He has an excellent speaking voice, a factor that helped launch him into broadcasting.) He later became a member of the Seattle Philharmonic Choral Society and then went into the armed service. At the age of twenty-seven, he decided to go to college. He enrolled at Seattle University and got a B.A. in history and then a master's degree in education. Phelps also has done work toward his Ph.D.

His education degree put him into teaching, first at the elementary level and then as one of the first black principals of a junior high school in the state of Washington. He taught at Bellevue, a white, upper- and middle-class suburb of Seattle.

"I had a good relationship with the kids, and I'm proud of it," Phelps said. "Most of them had many things, but not much in the way of values."

The assassination of Dr. Martin Luther King changed the direction of Phelps's life from education to broadcasting. There was a former college classmate of Dr. King in the Bellevue area, and Phelps, as principal, asked him to deliver the memorial address at the junior high school. But the man had a time conflict, so Don Phelps wrote and delivered the speech himself.

As it happened, the news media had selected the junior high as a focal point of coverage for King services. Phelps's address was considered the best in the entire Seattle area. It was carried on TV and radio and repeated again and again. KOMO ran it four times in two days because of the many requests for it.

The speech convinced Jack Eddy, KOMO-TV news director, that Phelps was a potentially fine broadcaster. He offered him a nightly spot, with carte blanche "to do your own thing." At this time, Phelps had been named assistant to the president of Bellevue Community College, and he hesitated about leaving this secure position to venture into the unfamiliar world of television. He compromised by going on the air two nights a week while retaining his full-time job. Eventually, however, he became a regular TV and radio broadcaster, a decision he has not regretted. To young blacks interested in a TV or radio news career, Phelps gave this advice:

"Get a college education and prepare by being a journalist. It's become a very professional field. Lots of black people could have my job, but they don't even know how to read. You have to be a logical thinker and express yourself clearly. You must have an interest in the world you live in, not in just one neighborhood or community. You have to have a high level of concern for what's going on in the world."

BELVA DAVIS

When she was writing a column for a California black weekly in 1961, Belva Davis thought she'd like to get into broadcasting. Besides, she needed an extra source of income. She finally landed a spot as a "what's going on around town" columnist for a small radio station, but there was a catch.

The job paid no salary. In a few months, the station manager gave her $5 a week for the program and she was on her way. A year later she got a better job with KDIA, a soul radio station in Oakland, California, while also serving as the station's traffic manager. She put in fourteen hours a day but managed to continue writing a column and acting as women's editor for the San Francisco *Sun-Reporter*, a black weekly.

Now a reporter for KPIX television in San Francisco and one of the best-known television personalities in town, Belva Davis is philosophical about her early struggles—struggles that really began with poverty, living in various ghetto sections of Oakland.

"I'm most thankful for the black media," she said. "Without it I would not have been even half ready when the white media decided to open its doors. Of course, I've run into every form of racism. The only difference is that longevity assures recognition, causing incidents of blatant bigotry to occur less often. In other words, I rarely have to show my press card to get into news conferences anymore."

In addition to her regular newscasts, Miss Davis has been active in community activities, winning a number of honors for her work on behalf of minority-group children. Zeta Phi Beta, a national collegiate sorority, named her "Woman of the Year" for her "contribution of time, talent and service to her community." She also has been named woman of the year by the *Sun-Reporter*, the Greyhound Bus Lines and the Texas College Alumni Association. She is a member of the "Focus on American Women" organized in twenty-one states to create better racial understanding, and she is active in the March of Dimes campaign.

A native of Monroe, Louisiana, Miss Davis grew up in

the Oakland area. She graduated from Berkeley High School but lack of money killed her plans for college and a teaching career. She later took a few courses at a local junior college, and her start in journalism came after several years of office work.

BLACK JOURNAL

A new concept in journalism is provided by *Black Journal,* a television series broadcast over the National Educational Television Network. It was conceived in April, 1968, following the murder of Dr. Martin Luther King, Jr., as a response to the growing mood for self-determination in the black communities of America. The program is advertised as being "for, by and about" black people and is produced by an all-black staff, which issued this comment:

"*Black Journal* seeks to fill an incredibly large gap in information about the black experience. While sensitizing all of the general public to issues and problems of African-Americans is a large concern, the show is primarily directed toward African-Americans. . . . Our staff is heavily committed to reflecting and realizing the needs of the black community. This cannot be achieved by addressing ourselves to a white audience, although they are welcome viewers, who, in fact, gain a more honest, accurate image of Black America. . . ."

The series has featured interviews with Huey Newton, of the Black Panthers, and Roy Innis, of CORE, developments in black theater, a special report on Biafra, a profile of movie director Melvin Van Peebles, a study of police attitudes and a look at Afro-American styles. *Black Journal* also has examined the need for more medical care in the ghettos and paid a tribute to the late Malcolm X.

The program has won several prizes, including the National Academy of Television Arts and Sciences award for outstanding achievement in magazine-type programming.

7 / Magazine Journalists

Magazines have one advantage over newspapers and television: they can be more easily geared to a particular readership. The newspaper and TV market is generally a mass audience. While there are mass-circulation magazines, a greater number are written and edited for special interest groups in such fields as sports, women's fashions, photography, travel, leisure, homecraft, culture, nature, politics, health, etc. For every *Life* there are hundreds of periodicals catering to readers with particular tastes. The specialized magazines appeal to advertisers who want their products displayed before potential consumers. The manufacturer of speed boats, for example, is unlikely to advertise them next to an afternoon soap opera on television. He will choose, instead, a sports magazine with strong masculine appeal. However, many advertisers prefer mass magazines because of the fact that they remain around a house or office for several weeks as a constant reminder of the products.

As to editorial content, magazines cover a wide range. Journalism is a term easily applied to such publications as *Time* and *Newsweek*, but a number of others fall into the same category. They include *Life, Ebony, Atlantic, Harper's, New Republic, Nation, National Review, New Yorker, Esquire* and more. Many magazine writers and editors came from the ranks of newspapers where they learned skills of great benefit to them in their new positions. For instance, the staffs of *Time* and *Newsweek* contain dozens of former newspaper reporters.

Blacks are serving on magazines, but not as widely as on newspapers. For some periodicals, tokenism is still the order of the day. Others will employ blacks simply as qualified staff members without reference to color. Blacks on today's magazines include the following:

ERNEST DUNBAR

Few journalists have led a more exciting life than Ernest Dunbar, who was senior editor of *Look* magazine. Essentially a writer and reporter, his assignments have taken him to the African rain forests, inside the Indian parliament and to Moscow and Montgomery, Alabama. He coordinated two special *Look* issues on Africa and wrote an exposé on the problems of African students in the Soviet Union. The latter won him an award from the Overseas Press Club for "Best Magazine Reporting From Abroad."

Dunbar joined *Look* in 1954 upon graduation from Temple University, where he received the Sigma Delta Chi award as the "outstanding male graduate in journalism" for that year and was editor-in-chief of the college newspaper. In 1957-58 he took a leave of absence from *Look* to do a year's graduate work in African studies at Northwestern University as a Mass Media Fellow of the Ford Foundation. He was senior editor from 1959 until the magazine ceased publication. In 1960 he accompanied Averell Harriman on a special fact-finding tour of Africa on behalf of the late John F. Kennedy, then the Democratic candidate for the presidency. *Look* assignments also took Dunbar to the Soviet Union, Poland, India, Germany and many other places.

Although regarded as an expert on African affairs, Ernest

Dunbar has written many articles on domestic issues, including the American Negro and race problems. His "Negro in America" piece has been widely reprinted and is included in the book *Race, Class and Power,* edited by Raymond W. Mack (American Book Company, 1963).

Dunbar has been honored by Lincoln University (Missouri) for outstanding journalistic work, and in 1968 he received a second Overseas Press Club award for an article on India's agricultural revolution. He also was appointed by the State Department's Advisory Council on Africa, a group set up to contribute to United States policy formation toward Africa.

Besides working for *Look*, Dunbar has been active in other media, including television. He was formerly moderator of "The World at Ten," a half-hour news analysis program on WNDT, New York's educational television station. He has written several magazine articles and is the author of a book, *The Black Expatriates*, a study of American Negroes living abroad.

Dunbar also is president of Black Perspective, a nationwide organization of black journalists concerned with bringing greater clarity and understanding to the coverage of racial news. Since *Look*'s demise, he has been doing freelance writing.

SAMUEL F. YETTE

Sam Yette is a correspondent in *Newsweek* magazine's Washington bureau, where he covers committee hearings and other House and Senate activities, particularly legislation affecting consumer affairs, education, welfare and housing.

A varied background in newspaper work, broadcast journalism and public relations has equipped Yette for his present assignments. Before going to *Newsweek* in 1968 he was a free-lance writer and consultant on public affairs and educational matters. From 1964 to 1967, he was executive officer of public affairs and special assistant to the director of the Office of Economic Opportunity in charge of civil rights programs. A year earlier he was information officer and then executive secretary of the Peace Corps.

Yette's newspaper experience has included science and aviation writing for the Dayton (Ohio) *Journal Herald* and Washington reporting for the Baltimore *Afro-American*. In 1956 he was a special assignment reporter for *Life* magazine and before that a sports announcer for WMFS radio in Chattanooga and a sports writer for the *Chattanooga Times*.

He is a native of Harriman, Tennessee, and was graduated from Tennessee A & I State University in Nashville with a degree in English. Four years later he received an M.A. in journalism and government from Indiana University. Tennessee A & I made him its "Alumnus of the Year" in 1964, and he is listed among the "Outstanding Young Men" of the National Junior Chamber of Commerce. Yette also is a member of Sigma Delta Chi and the Capital Press Club.

ALEX HALEY

Being a successful free-lance writer in America is a major journalistic accomplishment. There are only about 200 men and women in the United States who earn their full income from writing books and magazine articles. One of them is Alex Haley, who was born in New York, reared in Tennessee and now lives in San Francisco.

Haley's biggest book is *The Autobiography of Malcolm X*, which has sold over three and one-half million copies and has been translated into eight languages since it was first published in 1965. It also has been named among the "Ten Best American Books of the 1960's Decade" and has earned other awards. The book grew out of a series of interviews Haley did for *Playboy* magazine. Among the leading personalities he questioned was the controversial Malcolm X, who agreed to have the magazine piece expanded into a book. Haley spent two years with the black leader in gathering material.

Alex Haley also has contributed to numerous other magazines, including *Harper's, Atlantic Monthly, The New York Times Magazine* and *Reader's Digest*, where he has been a staff writer and roving correspondent.

He began writing articles in the Coast Guard, which he joined in 1939 after finishing high school and two years of college. He always had been fascinated by books of adventure, and the Coast Guard gave him the opportunity for travel and the time to write. When his watch was over, he wrote late into the night aboard the various ships on which he sailed. In 1949 the Coast Guard adopted a new rating—journalist—for Haley. Three years later he was advanced to Chief Journalist and began handling the United States Coast Guard's public relations. He continued to free-lance, and after eight years of effort small magazines began accepting his manuscripts. Haley retired from the Coast Guard in 1959 after twenty years' service and began writing full-time. He also began a remarkable research project into his own background. With only slender oral clues passed on to him by his maternal grandmother, Haley managed to trace her side of the family back to a Mandingo youth named Kunta Kinte, from the small village of Juffurein in Gambia, West Africa. Kunta, who was Haley's seventh-generation forefather, was sold into slavery and transported to Colonial America on the

American slaveship *Lord Ligonier*, which arrived in Annapolis, Maryland, on September 29, 1767.

No writer researches for fun, and Haley is no exception. He wrote a book on his findings entitled *Before This Anger*, which was made into a movie filmed on location in Gambia, England and America.

In addition to his writing, the forty-nine-year-old Haley teaches a course, Black Heritage, at the University of California at Berkeley.

In the final stages of writing *Before This Anger*, Haley found it almost impossible to work at home because of ringing telephones and other distractions. He telephoned a freighter company and asked if it had any ship going anywhere for a full summer. As it happened, the Norwegian freighter *M/S Villanger* was leaving for a three-month trip around South America. Haley promptly packed his bags and got aboard. He holed up in his cabin and wrote fourteen hours a day, emerging only for meals.

"One must cultivate an unusual capacity for self-discipline to be a writer," Haley declared. "You must make yourself work, for yourself, longer and harder than anyone else would ever ask you to work. I worked, learning every day, seven days a week for eight years, before selling my first article. I don't know how I sustained that long a period, except that I loved trying to write. That love is still with me."

LERONE BENNETT, JR.

Lerone Bennett is a man who combines journalism and history and has the best of both worlds. He is senior editor of *Ebony* magazine and has written six scholarly books and a number of poems, short stories and articles. His book *Before the Mayflower: A History of the Negro in America, 1619-*

1966, is considered an outstanding historical treatment and is used as a text in several Black Studies courses. He also authored *The Negro Mood, What Manner of Man: A Biography of Martin Luther King, Jr., Black Power, U.S.A., The Human Side of Reconstruction, 1867-1877* and *Pioneers in Protest.* His books have been translated into French, German, Japanese, Swedish and Arabic.

Lerone Bennett went to work as a newspaperman after attending public schools in Jackson, Mississippi, and graduating from Morehouse College with a B.A. degree. He was a reporter for the black Atlanta *Daily World* from 1949 to 1952, when he became city editor. In that same year he became associate editor of *Jet* magazine, and in 1954 he switched to *Ebony.* Bennett has traveled extensively in Europe and Africa and has lectured before many audiences in the United States.

JAMES BENNETT CONAWAY

At the age of twenty-nine, James Conaway was delivering packages around New York City for $50 a week. Today, at forty, he is an associate editor of *Fortune* magazine, one of the top jobs in journalism. For Conaway, it has been a long, hard road. Being black was only one of the problems he encountered along the way.

Things started out fairly well for him at Boys High School in Brooklyn, New York. He was a member of the school's world record 440-yard relay team. At the same time, he was interested in music and was playing in a symphony orchestra and marching band. On weekends he earned spending money by playing jazz on his vibraphone with small combos. And he wrote short articles for the school newspaper.

His athletic prowess (he made the *Look* All-American Track Team in 1948) brought him a shower of scholarship offers from colleges around the country. He eventually accepted a four-year scholarship to Colby College, Waterville, Maine, but was forced to leave in his freshman year because of illness. Later he began again at Adelphi College, Garden City, New York, on another scholarship, but ill luck continued to dog him. His funds ran out, and he had to leave a year before completing the requirement for a degree.

"The next years were difficult," he remembered. "Without a college degree I might have obtained a job as a reporter on a newspaper. But in the mid-'50s I was still somewhat naïve about my opportunities in the American business world. There were no openings on the major New York newspapers for me as a cub, and the Negro papers had their own mysterious clique."

What followed was a series of jobs, mostly menial and/or low-paying. For a brief time he was a special assistant to the head writer for NBC's "Today Show," but there was a staff cut and he wound up in the mailroom. "I took what I could get," Conaway recalled. This also included being a driver's helper on a Railway Express truck and the aforementioned package delivery job. In 1966 he returned to school and got his bachelor's degree in black history from Goddard College in Vermont.

Conaway was thirty years old when he got his first job in journalism—as a proofreader for the New York Academy of Sciences.

"It was a nonprofit organization that gave me an opportunity to learn and advance until becoming one of its associate editors within two years," he said. This experience led to a writer's position with *Long Lines* magazine, an American Telephone & Telegraph Company publication.

From there he went to *Fortune,* a Time, Inc., magazine dealing with the world of business and finance.

Conaway is philosophical about the length of time it took to achieve his current status. He said:

I'm not resentful that positions with major publications were not available to me ten years earlier. I do think that though prejudices of all kinds will still be with us in the future, rejection of the complete system is not a mature attitude. Nobody has a priority on hate. Feeling hated, I returned what I thought was hate from white people, but was actually something worse—indifference. I have long since tempered my frustrations of ten or fifteen years ago. It's more to the point to say that nobody has a priority on talent, effort or ambition. These are spread far and wide. In the face of opinion to the contrary, I would like to continue proving just that. As an associate editor of *Fortune,* I have never been treated overtly different from any other member of the staff. It is hard work most of the time, but it's not a picnic for my colleagues either—and that's the way we like it.

ERNEST HOLSENDOLPH

Conaway is one of two black associate editors at *Fortune.* The other is Ernest Holsendolph, who came to the magazine after working for the *Cleveland Press* and the *Washington Star,* both dailies, as education writer and general reporter. He had been encouraged to follow a writing career by his high school journalism teacher in Cleveland. While still in high school Holsendolph sent unsolicited movie and television reviews to the newspapers, some of which were printed.

After graduating from Columbia College in New York, he got his first news job with the Cleveland *Call & Post*, a black weekly. Four months later the *Press*, where he had first tried, said it had an opening for him. Musing over his professional life, Holsendolph said:

"I don't know how I came about my ambition in journalism. It did not come directly from my parents—a father who grew up as a Georgia farmer and raised me and three sisters on a Cleveland laborer's pay, nor my mother, who helped me through school on her earnings as a domestic. By whatever means I found my path, I'm glad I came this way."

GEORGE E. CURRY

When a top athlete winds up as a sports reporter for a leading sports magazine, he is most likely enjoying his work. This is true of George Curry, reporter for *Sports Illustrated*, who has written stories on baseball, basketball, football and track.

It would be hard to find someone better qualified in terms of background and training. In Tuscaloosa, Alabama, his home town, he began playing basketball with older boys in a housing project court. At Druid High School he was quarterback of the football team and treasurer of the student government association and was selected as "Best All-Around Senior."

He entered Knoxville College, in Tennessee, where he combined football and journalism. He was editor-in-chief of the school newspaper and quarterback and captain of the gridiron team, and he was elected to "Who's Who Among Students in American Universities and Colleges." Curry also managed to become a campus correspondent for the *National Observer* and was named to the college's board of trustees. He joined *Sports Illustrated* immediately after his graduation.

Discussing his work, Curry said:

"Basically, sports writing is no different from any other type of writing. It requires certain fundamental skills. But it does allow more latitude than in straight news writing. Newspaper reporters, for instance, are usually limited to sticking to the hard facts: what happened? when? why?, etc. But a sports writer is a critic as well as a reporter. He can say, 'John Doe did poorly and should not have been in the game.' Then, too, he can delve into the personality, problems, beliefs and off-field activities of a particular player. In other words, we have more flexibility."

Such flexibility has allowed Curry to travel all over the country in search of sports stories. He has been active on *Sports Illustrated*'s annual college football and basketball issues, in which reporters attempt to determine the best twenty teams in the United States. "It's fun at the season's end to check your predictions against the final standings," he remarked.

George Curry has this message for those who want to be sports writers:

"In addition to learning all you can about sports, read, read, read! You can never read enough. Try to avoid the pitfall of attempting to specialize at an early age. That is, don't say you're going to be a pro football or pro basketball writer. If you're fortunate enough to get a job with a reputable publication, you'll be required to do a multiplicity of things. So learn as much as you can about everything you can."

The young sports writer said his favorite story in *Sports Illustrated* concerned Kevin Knox, an eleven-year-old track star who ran the mile in 5:03. Curry said he works constantly to hone and refine his style.

"It's important that a writer write," he emphasized. "No one will ever know you're a writer unless you write. Write at every opportunity—for the school paper, essays, poetry, anything that will keep you writing. Ask the teacher to look at your work, and then request his opinion. Ask for suggestions, and constantly re-evaluate your progress. Don't try to copy anyone's style. You should observe what noted writers do well, but ultimately you must develop a style that is unique."

Curry said that the young writer, in addition to perfecting his style, should have confidence in himself. "In order to be successful," he said, "one must feel that he is the best in the business and strive to be just that. There is no substitute for self-confidence. If you don't believe in yourself, you're already defeated."

While on *Sports Illustrated*, Curry has found time to write a book on Jake Gaither, a Florida A & M University coach.

JACOB E. SIMMS

When Jacob Simms graduated from Winston-Salem State College in North Carolina, there was little hope of a career in journalism, despite his interest in writing. He settled instead for a teaching career, eventually getting his master's degree. Throughout this time, he never lost his interest in journalism and often discussed the matter with his wife, also a teacher.

"She encouraged me to make the attempt," Simms said. "Her reasoning was that if I did not succeed, I could return to the classroom, since my teaching certificate was still valid. But if the experiment worked, I'd be on my way at last."

The experiment worked. Simms is currently a correspondent for *Time* magazine in Chicago. The road he took to get there was a long and hard one, beginning in Charlotte, North Carolina. One August day he walked into the lobby of the *Charlotte Observer* to inquire about a job. He waited at the counter for several minutes before he was approached by a young white girl, who asked what she could do for him.

"I told her I had come to apply for work," Simms said.

"I'm sorry, but we don't have any routes open right now," the receptionist replied. "Would you care to come back at a later date? But call before you come."

"I told her that I hadn't come to apply for a paper route but for a job as a reporter," Simms recounted.

This threw the girl into a spin, and she hurried away to a glass-lined office in the rear. She returned in a few minutes with the personnel manager, who introduced himself and then asked Simms who or what organization had sent him.

"No one sent me," Simms answered. "I'm on my own."

When the personnel man recovered from his surprise, he handed Simms an application form. But it wasn't until three interviews later that he was finally hired on the copy desk of the *Observer*.

Before starting work he was approached by the managing editor, who told him: "I must warn you that this is the toughest spot in the newsroom because you have the last contact with the paper." (Copy editors put headlines on stories and check them for accuracy, style, grammar and spelling before they go to the printer.)

"Also," the editor continued, "we'll find out very quickly if journalism is for you and if you are for journalism. Want to try?"

When Simms replied affirmatively, the editor said: "We

add only one thing. If at any point you decided that you can't make it, you will tell us. If we decide that you just aren't going to work out, we'll tell you. Agreed?"

Jacob Simms agreed, and he was put to work part-time to permit him to retain his teaching position in case the *Observer* trial did not pan out. Gradually his stint was increased to twenty hours a week and then to full time. The only caution given him was to slow down, because he was doing more than his share of the work. In addition to editing copy, he wrote news stories, editorials and book reviews. During this period, Simms recalled, he received praise and encouragement from the *Observer*'s publisher, C. A. "Pete" McKnight.

Simms said that he lost his temper only once on the newspaper. He had made friends with the white staff members of the copy desk, and the group would frequently dine together on their meal breaks. One night, as he was returning from dinner with the group, he found a packet of Ku Klux Klan literature on the front seat of his car with this note: "Give this to your nigger-loving friends."

Simms reported the incident to the *Observer* management, who traced the packet to two men who worked in the newspaper's print shop. They were told that if they did anything like that again they would be fired without explanation.

"I never got anymore Klan stuff," Simms said. "I was most gratified by the response of management to this situation."

Simms left the *Observer* to accept a *Time* fellowship to the Columbia University Graduate School of Journalism, where he earned another master's degree. He joined *Time* shortly after. Speaking about his work for *Time*, he said:

Thus far I've been successful in avoiding the role of black specialist for the magazine. I detest the tendency

of some people in the press to lean on "experts." There
are no such animals as "black experts"; certainly there
are no white experts. If there were, he or she would
probably have to be black.

Although I do not consider myself to be a crusader in
the loudest manner possible, there is a certain function
that I can and sometimes do perform for *Time*. I bring
to the magazine a certain sensitivity or feeling for minority stories that they would not otherwise get. I enjoy
my work at *Time* because they honor one of the basic
tenets of my employment: that I do not become a black
reporter. I consider myself a journalist, and I am competitive.

The *Time* writer said that he is a realist about his job.
"Being black may have gotten me hired," he declared, "but
it won't keep me from getting fired. Being black today is an
advantage, although the basic premise remains: black or
not, you have to produce. Despite the high ideology of
journalism, it's still a business in the American tradition of
profit making. Any journalist who thinks that he doesn't
have to make a contribution in terms of his best effort is
fooling himself. I acknowledge the debt I owe to the blacks
who threw bricks and marched. They opened the door for
me. But the fact stands: I had to walk through by myself.
And if I am to stay with *Time*, I must produce.

"This point about producing is one that I would advise
young blacks interested in journalism to consider carefully.
A black newspaper owner will fire them just as quickly if
they are nonproductive."

According to Simms, the black journalist is in a unique
position. He can use his position to educate the public, or
he can "do his own thing."

"It would seem to me," the journalist observed, "that it would be more worthwhile to use the position to promote understanding and appreciation of the differences in people. The racial conflict in this country will never be resolved until people stop talking *at* each other and starting talking *to* each other. No amount of rhetoric will wash away this fact."

Simms warned young people against going into journalism if they are interested only in the glamorous aspects of the field. "Journalism," he noted, "offers a lot of heartbreak and disappointment; it's a lot of hard work, a lot of tears and responsibility. But it also gives much satisfaction to one who applies himself diligently. It is a good feeling to do a thankless job well, to get the story despite all the obstacles.

"A sense of diplomacy and skill in questioning people is necessary, too. Simply having a hairdo, knowing the handshakes, wearing the tribal garb and waving a steno pad is not enough. There is more to being black than a hairdo and a handshake. Have the patience to thrash out the details and facts, and acquire a devotion to these facts."

LAWRENCE PATRICK PATTERSON

One of the most exciting facets of journalism is to be connected with a new magazine or newspaper. "Pat" Patterson has had both experiences. He is currently editor of *Black Enterprise,* a slick-paper magazine that covers the progress and developments of blacks in the business world. The young periodical has a circulation of more than 100,000 black businessmen and women.

Previously, Patterson had been managing editor of the

Manhattan Tribune, a weekly designed to create a dialogue between blacks and whites. He also has been editor of a black weekly, the *New York Courier.*

Patterson got his start in the newspaper business. After taking his degree in journalism at New York University, he became a supervisor in the New York City Welfare Department. In 1963 he became one of the first black reporters on *Newsday,* where he won two awards for outstanding reporting: the Paul Tobenkin and the Society of Silurians awards. The latter is an organization of professional newsmen.

As the editor of *Black Enterprise,* Pat Patterson is still very much a reporter. He tracks down ideas for articles, writing some of them himself and assigning others to staff members. Although published in New York, the magazine roams far and wide in search of material. Stories have centered around a black clothier in Los Angeles, a program by the General Electric Company to launch blacks into their own electronic companies and a black-owned meat-processing firm in Cleveland. The magazine also carries articles about black businesses that failed and why.

Pat Patterson also has a deep interest in the gains made by blacks in journalism. He has taught a course for black student journalists at New York University and has advised many others on career matters. He believes that it is very important for the white media to increase the number of blacks they are hiring. He said:

Before 1963 there was a handful of black journalists working on white-owned daily newspapers. They were rarer still on radio and television. Then came the rebellions, and the search was on for black talent. The search was to continue for nearly five years as city after city was convulsed by racial disorders. Some of the blacks hired during that period were talented; others were not.

Tragically, however, it was the American people, black and white, who were the losers. Because there were too few trained black journalists and a smaller number of whites who understood the black experience, much of that period from the mid to late 1960s begged for positive interpretation. The 1970s will be even more demanding for the black journalist. We are moving, as the Kerner report indicated, toward two societies—one black, the other white, separate and unequal. Our cities are getting blacker as the suburbs grow whiter. Future reporting, therefore, will require not only knowledge but sensitivity and understanding.

Patterson urged young black journalists to interpret the black experience not only to black America but to white America as well, revealing the nation as a whole with all its positives and contradictions. He stated:

Though black pride is most welcomed and desirable, it is not enough simply to bask in the sun of newly found awareness. This will not broaden any tax base, create new jobs or build needed housing. In my opinion, if black journalists are to make a real contribution, they must not confine their interest solely to so-called black issues, although it is vitally important that they know and understand as much as possible about the black struggle in the United States and the world.

Black journalists in the white media, it seems to me, have the hardest job, whether it be in the handling of white or black news. In the first instance their competence may be questioned; in the second, their loyalty. A black journalist is, after all, black. Still, there is no substitute for excellence. And he must strive always to achieve that goal. He should no more compromise his skills than he would his blackness.

AUDREEN BALLARD

"Today there is nothing more important to blacks than communications." These are the words of Audreen Ballard, an editor in the articles department of *Redbook* magazine, whose content is slanted for women between eighteen and thirty-four years old.

Mrs. Ballard has been working in communications since she graduated from Cheyney State Teachers College in Pennsylvania. "My career in journalism began," she said, "when a feisty black editor of the *Philadelphia Independent*, a black weekly, snarlingly decided to take a chance on my eagerness and my annoyingly apparent fascination with the printed word, and hire me as a reporter. I am greatly indebted to him."

The young reporter covered police courts, politics and civil rights assignments that offered little glamour, plenty of hard work and useful insight into the mechanism of the inner city.

"It was also a bit risky," Mrs. Ballard remembers. "In one instance I was the only black reporter on a story about white home owners maddened by the rumor of the first black family to move into their neighborhood. It was, nonetheless, a valuable experience."

Mrs. Ballard is a strong advocate of newspaper experience as training for any kind of communications work. She explained:

"The variety, the flow and flux of general assignment reporting increases your understanding of people, issues and systems. This, in turn, gives you a broad-based foundation from which to develop a sense of news values, confidence in your own judgment and a sense of responsibility for a humane black value system that will withstand the culturally determined charge of objectivity. As a black journalist, these qualities will stand you in good stead whether you work with such Establishment institutions as *Ebony, The New York Times*, NBC or decide to devote your talents to developing alternatives to these publications."

The magazine editor said it's a good idea for young journalists to "hone their skills to a fine point."

"Copy editing may be a drag, but it's a necessary skill and discipline that, mastered in school and early job training, will allow you to expend your time and energies in more creative and exploratory directions." She added that this is especially important for black writers and editors.

"The fact that the media have frequently been derelict in honestly reporting and interpreting news crucial to us is only one indication of the need for improvement," she asserted. "We must not only determine systems for getting the word to blacks from San Francisco through to St. Louis, Newark and Philadelphia on a sustained basis, but more importantly we must credibly and responsibly *interpret* it in all its ramifications. There is much that must be recorded, and there is some journalistic outlet for you, whatever your point of view. If not, you'll make one."

Before joining *Redbook* in 1969, Mrs. Ballard was a public relations representative for the Columbia Record Club and a writer for WFIL radio in Philadelphia. She is active in community activities and is a member of Black Perspective, an organization of black journalists.

JOHN L. DOTSON, JR.

When he was in high school in Paterson, New Jersey, John Dotson's English teacher suggested that he enroll in her journalism class. He did and found he really liked it, particularly working for the school newspaper. He's been a journalist ever since.

Today he is *Newsweek* magazine's bureau chief in Los Angeles, a job that takes him all over the Pacific Coast and beyond. He has covered an infinite variety of stories, including riots in Detroit, Cleveland, Newark, Jersey City and New York; the 1968 Democratic Convention disturbances; the Big Three auto negotiations; and the Lockheed loan guarantee controversy.

After graduating from Temple University with a degree in journalism, Dotson was a reporter for five years with the *Newark News* and then spent a year with the *Detroit Free Press* before joining *Newsweek*.

"To black youngsters thinking about a career in journalism, I say right on," Dotson declared. "It is one of the few jobs that is both enjoyable and important. Opportunities for enjoyment—be they forced or natural—are there in greater numbers than in most other fields, I believe. But the competition is rough. Journalism attracts exceedingly bright, driving young whites, many with outstanding talent. A good, rounded educational background and an expansive reading list are important."

Dotson, however, has reservations about the role of the black man in major media.

"He is in a difficult position," the *Newsweek* writer said. "All too often a black is employed solely to cover ghetto affairs when he is anxious to prove his worth as a general reporter. When he scores well in the ghetto, editors attribute his success to his being black, rather than to his ability as a reporter. Once he breaks out of that bag, a black reporter can feel surer about his talents and probably do a better all-around job.

"This doesn't mean blacks don't want to cover the black community when there is an important story to be done. It is then that a black reporter feels he has something special to add to the reporting—a sensitivity and understanding that most whites lack."

Dotson warned that blacks employed by white media must expect some criticism and hostility from the black community no matter how well they report black affairs.

"The feeling among their black brothers is that they work for the Establishment," Dotson said. "The critics contend that a black newsman can't really tell it like it is. If he did, they say, the Establishment press wouldn't print it. It is a difficult criticism for the black to rectify. In the end, the question boils down to this: 'Am I doing more for my people and the cause in this position, or would I do better doing something else?' "

RUTH N. ROSS

In *Newsweek*'s New York office Ruth Ross is considered one of the best reporters on the staff. With the title of New York Correspondent, she covers mainly black affairs, an assignment that takes her up and down the East Coast. She has covered the Bobby Seale trial and that of the so-called Panther 13, among other stories.

A native New Yorker, Miss Ross was hired by *Newsweek* as a researcher in 1964. She had been assistant editor of

Electronics Design, a trade magazine, and had worked for a book publisher after her graduation from Hunter College with a degree in English. In 1966 *Newsweek* made her an assistant editor, with reporting assignments for the magazine's departments of medicine, religion and music.

Three years later she left the magazine to become Editor-in-Chief of *Essence,* a new magazine for black women. The idea for the publication had been conceived by Miss Ross, who also gave it its name. As the first editor, she joined the drive to obtain supporting funds for *Essence* and also organized the editorial staff. Seventeen black reporters and editors from white magazines gave up secure jobs to take the risk of working for a new magazine.

"I told them they were taking a gamble, but they came anyway," Ruth Ross recalled. "They really wanted to see *Essence* succeed. A tremendous amount of effort, pain and agony went into the magazine, but it was an experience I treasure."

Miss Ross returned to *Newsweek* in 1970, deciding that news reporting, rather than women's features, was what she liked best. She said she prefers concentrating on black stories because "I feel it is my duty. I can give stories a black perspective that they might otherwise not have."

She suggested that young blacks aiming for her field first acquire the skills. "If they can get journalism education, they should by all means," she continued. "I can remember interviewing many young blacks for jobs in communications. They brought with them a beautiful, marvelous sense of blackness but no usable skills. They must have training or experience under their belts before they apply for media jobs."

Miss Ross said that beginners must make their own choice between white or black publications, but she added that "a certain percentage of us have to stay with the Establishment magazines and newspapers to give a black point of view to these publications. Some blacks can then take their skills to the black media, which are needed to present our version of the truth."

8 / Public Relations and Advertising—The Image Makers

To many people the name Madison Avenue conveys a picture of well-dressed public relations (P.R.) and advertising men negotiating multimillion-dollar contracts over lavish lunches at plush restaurants. There's some truth to this idea, but it overlooks one important element. These men and women are highly skilled professionals who work long and hard on the accounts they handle. Moreover, they are in a highly competitive business in which the loss of a single client can mean the difference between success and failure.

Both public relations and advertising require communication skills, but there is one key difference. Advertisers must pay for space in newspapers and magazines or for air time on radio or television. The public relations man, on the other hand, tries to get his client's message into the papers and over the air without paying one cent. If the message is newsworthy, interesting, entertaining or all three, he has a good chance of getting free publicity. Newspaper and broadcast news editors cannot possibly cover all events, so they rely on P.R. firms to supply them with material. Thus, if the public relations department of a pharmaceutical firm sends out a release on a new drug, it will most likely be used by the news media. The same would be true of an automobile company announcing a new safety device to reduce accidents.

Until a few years ago, Madison Avenue was a white enclave, except for a few black public relations and advertising firms in New York and elsewhere. There has been no

153

major change, but black faces are appearing in a number
of white companies throughout the United States. A few
blacks hold executive positions, and their number is growing. With some clients reaping as much as 40 per cent of their
profits from the black community, the agencies saw the light
and began to employ blacks. At the same time, black P.R.
and advertising firms are increasing.

An investigation by the New York City Commission on
Human Rights showed that in 1967-68 a total of 492 blacks
and 199 Puerto Ricans were employed by the top twelve
New York advertising agencies. This was a minority percentage of 5.6 of the total work force of 12,206. Two years later,
the commission reported, the twelve firms employed 1,015
blacks (8.4 per cent) and 550 Puerto Ricans (2.9 per cent)
of their total 12,123 employees. The figures included a hike
from 135 to 355 in professional categories (account executives, copywriters, artists, etc.), or 5.4 per cent. In 1967-68,
the number was 1.9 per cent for minority groups in professional or top level posts.

Black Enterprise magazine reported in its February, 1971,
issue:

Madison Avenue is changing. The new era is not only re-
flected in the demise of the gray flannel suit, with ad-
men now leaning toward bold, garishly mod fashions.
It is also apparent in the increasing number of black
faces in the bustling offices where small groups of men
devise the slogans they hope will mold then remold eat-
ing, drinking and dress preferences all over the world.
It is apparent in the watering holes that cater to advertising people where confident black executives gulp
scotch while they authoritatively discuss accounts and
billings, the adman's reason for living. Some of the

Madison Avenue newcomers are account executives, writers and art directors for agencies with multimillion-dollar billings. Others operate their own agencies. Although they are still relatively few in number, the rise of blacks to the executive level in the $20 billion-a-year industry is a dramatic improvement over the positions held by blacks just a few years ago. . . .

Here are portraits of some of the black executives in public relations and advertising.

DOUGLASS L. ALLIGOOD

Doug Alligood, who ranks among the most successful of New York advertising men, believes strongly in two principles:

1. Advertising agencies and corporations should employ more blacks and members of other minority groups.

2. There are many blacks now in high school and college who are good recruiting prospects for this field.

Alligood is in a position to know. The black executive is manager of general advertising for RCA in New York. In this position he is responsible to the director of corporate advertising for evaluation, development and implementation of advertising programs involving corporate headquarters and RCA's divisions and subsidiary activities. He was given the title in 1971 after nine years with the big advertising agency of Batten, Barton, Durstine & Osborn, Inc., ending up as an account executive. During his agency career he was responsible for such large advertising accounts as New York Telephone, Delta Airlines, the duPont Company, Campbell Soup and Schafer Beer.

Doug Alligood speaks frankly about his business and attitudes toward it. He told a white advertising group:

Unfortunately for those of us in advertising, there is a feeling among many whites that blacks with the qualifications for advertising jobs are difficult, if not almost impossible, to find. Many of these same whites also believe that the nature of the advertising business calls for a diversity of business background and education, more so than many other kinds of business—and that these qualifications are more commonly found among whites rather than blacks.

Assuming for the moment that this once was true—today things are different. There are young black people in colleges all across the land—and youngsters moving from high school to college—providing a vast reservoir of the kind of talent needed in advertising. . . . For the most part, minority-group people know that there are few barriers in teaching and civil service careers because of race. But they are not aware of opportunities in advertising, and few consider advertising a career.

The general misconception of what a job in advertising involves produces a real credibility gap. Because minority-group people don't imagine they can establish careers in advertising, they do not even consider it in their vocational planning. . . . The advertising business exists on talent. The only way we can keep our business from falling into the doldrums of mediocrity is to make the business attractive to new sources of talents —minority-group people. But before we get them into the personnel offices, we have to convince them that the effort is worthwhile. . . .

Alligood was one of the founders of the Group for Advertising Progress (GAP), whose main goal is to advance the social and economic status of minority-group persons in the fields of advertising, radio, television and the communication arts. The predominantly black organization encourages ad organizations to hire more minority people and works to improve the standing of those already working in the field. GAP also seeks to spread the word among minority youngsters that employment and training opportunities do exist in communications. The group's slogan is borrowed from black Mayor Richard Hatcher, of Gary, Indiana: "For God's sake, let us get together!"

Said Alligood: "GAP is not, nor do we intend to become, an employment agency. Our desire is to help put people in touch." To this end, GAP has sent its members into high schools and colleges with large minority-group populations to discuss advertising careers with students. It also has assisted the Urban League in its summer workshop program for minority-group teachers and has sponsored creative workshops for training blacks and Puerto Ricans in television advertising. The students learned, among other things, how a television commercial is produced—from rough "storyboard" to the finished print. Professional art directors, writers and producers volunteered their services as instructors.

Alligood pointed out that good jobs exist in advertising for those who have not attended college but are talented in art and writing.

"The climate of advertising is changing," he explained. "Where once many ad men were hired because of their social and college backgrounds, today, more and more, people are hired for their own talents."

Alligood's talents began to show at Bradley University, Peoria, Illinois, where he got a bachelor of fine arts degree in 1956. Following a three-year tour as an Air Force officer, he worked for WCHB radio in Detroit and then joined the staff of BBD&O in 1962 as an account representative for

Dodge cars and trucks, Pepsi-Cola and Ford's Autolite division.

Would he want his children to enter advertising? He replied: "To me, advertising embodies all of the things that we normally associate with a desirable career. It's exciting, it's challenging, it's rewarding and sometimes it's even fun. I don't mean that it's a perfect business—far from it. There are many areas that need to be improved, particularly in minority-group employment and advancement, opportunities for women and our general public image among others. But advertising is a living, constantly changing, vital industry that welcomes and thrives on new ideas. Where else can bright, young people express themselves in a positive manner as they do on Madison Avenue?

"Would I want my children to enter advertising? The question is academic. The only things I want for my children are continued good health, strength of character and equal opportunity to develop their talents to the limits of their abilities. No matter what careers they choose, I hope they enjoy them as much as I do mine."

TOM L. SIMS

As a highly successful advertising and marketing specialist, Tom Sims invites young graduates to enter the business world. Sims, vice-president of the Strategy Workshop, a division of Interpublic, Inc., in New York, declared:

"The young graduate going into business today is entering a world that can only be called extremely nervous—and the accelerating pressure for change from all sides is steadily increasing the nervousness. At the same time, these same pressures for change are making the business world extremely exciting.

"I would say to the young graduate: Think more of the excitement than the nervousness; remember that you, as a young graduate, are part of one of the pressures, and you're in prime position to help make some of that positive change.

"And, if that young graduate happens to be black, I'd add this: That business world is a little bit more afraid of you than it is of others—a bit more nervous about you. But business is becoming increasingly aware that it *needs* you; you bring something to it that it has to have if it's going to change in a positive direction. And it needs you as you are, along with what you have learned. So adapt to it, but remain yourself."

A graduate of Hampton Institute, Sims began his career at Elmer Roper & Associates, a New York–based market and opinion research firm (the Roper Poll). He then moved to BBD&O as a marketing specialist, primarily in packaged goods. From there he went to another leading advertising firm, McCann-Erickson, Inc., becoming a vice-president in 1967. In his present position Sims's responsibilities include devising marketing strategies, new product planning and other areas of corporate planning and business systems.

Tom Sims has a number of outside activities. Among other things he is a member of the board of the Interracial Council for Business Opportunity.

A. ALEXANDER MORISEY

"The need for communication skills cannot be overstated as a grounding for public relations," said Alex Morisey, public relations manager of *The New York Times* and a veteran of several years of P.R. and newspaper work.

Morisey should know. He began as the North Carolina bureau manager for the Norfolk (Virginia) *Journal and*

Guide, traveling through the state on news assignments. In 1949 he made history by becoming the first black reporter for the white Winston-Salem *Journal* and Twin City *Sentinel* and most likely the first black man to work for any white Southern newspaper. Morisey covered mostly black news, but also wrote book reviews, sports and other items. He remained there until 1955, when he became director of special publicity for the American Friends Service Committee in Philadelphia. Among his responsibilities was that of editing a quarterly publication reaching about 70,000 readers, and writing a weekly newsletter. One year he was sent to Austria to gather field material on a Quaker program to aid Hungarian refugees after the uprising against the Russians.

Alex Morisey's work with the Quakers led to his next job as director of public relations and research for the city of Philadelphia's Commission on Human Relations. In this capacity he wrote, edited and produced pamphlets and other informational materials as well as being responsible for a monthly newsletter, news releases and radio and TV spot announcements.

Before going to the *Times* in 1969, Morisey was director of public relations for Howard University, including the school's sports programs. In addition, he supervised productions of university radio and television shows.

One of his main interests at the *Times* is a program to improve student newspapers in high schools and colleges. His office provides resource materials to improve journalism education and furnishes speakers from the *Times* editorial staff. Largely through Morisey's efforts, a special college course to train high school journalism teachers and newspaper advisers has been offered at New York University. The program also has the support of the Newspaper Fund, a Dow-Jones–supported foundation to support journalism education.

Morisey is on the board of directors of the New York chapter of the Public Relations Society of America. He also is a member of the National and Capital Press Clubs in Washington, D.C.

A native of North Carolina, he holds a bachelor of science degree from Shaw University in Raleigh, and has done graduate study at the American University in Washington.

WALTER CHRISTMAS

Newspaper reporting has been the starting point for a number of public relations executives. The newsman is considered a good bet for P.R. work because of his sense of what editors want. He can also communicate information in newspaper style—the main element in the first paragraph and the other aspects of the story in descending order of importance.

Walter Christmas, director of public relations for the Coca-Cola Bottling Company of New York, Inc., had this background—and more. He was a newspaper reporter, produced company magazines and was a free-lance writer. Before joining Coca-Cola, he was director of urban affairs at Ruder & Finn, the world-wide public relations firm in New York. While there he organized a national network of black P.R. firms which enabled his firm to work more effectively for clients in programs relating to minority and community affairs. Christmas also taught a public-relations class at New York University.

Among his Ruder & Finn clients were Hunt-Wesson Foods, Scripto, Manpower, Huntington National Bank, Bristol-Myers, Clairol, Philip Morris, Mind, Inc., and many others.

At one time in his career Christmas was managing editor of Educational Heritage, a publishing company which put out a ten-volume series on black history. He also was executive director of the American Foundation on Non-Violence, an organization founded by the late Dr. Martin Luther King, Jr. In addition, the P.R. executive was the first American press officer for the Ghana Information and Trade Center after that West African nation achieved its independence.

ROY EATON

How does one become vice-president and music director for a major advertising firm, such as Benton & Bowles, Inc.? Well, if you're Roy Easton, who happens to hold that position, you are a talented, versatile musician who made a piano debut with the Chicago Symphony Orchestra.

Eaton, who joined Benton & Bowles in 1959, is responsible for all music connected with his firm's radio and television commercials. He prepared for his duties by composing TV commercial jingles himself and was formerly copywriter in charge of radio and TV music at Young & Rubicam, another large ad agency.

But Eaton can easily prove that he is a serious musician as well. He has recorded three albums under the Mace label. On two, "Bach Trio Sonatas" and "The Rococo Flute," he performs on the harpsichord. On the third—contemporary chamber music—he is featured on the piano. He has taught piano at both the City College of New York and the Manhattan School of Music. Even that doesn't tell the whole story of his versatility. He also has recorded two pop albums, "The Lotus Palace" and "Turn In, Turn On."

Roy Eaton is a graduate of the Music & Art High School in New York and holds a bachelor of social science degree from City College, where he graduated magna cum laude. He then got his master's degree in music from Yale. In his junior year in college he won the Aaron Naumburg Award for a year's study abroad, which he spent at the University of Zurich and the Conservatory of Lucerne in Switzerland. He was the winner of the first Kosciuszko Foundation Chopin Award for pianists and the Nathaniel Currier and Junior Sterling Fellowships from Yale. Eaton is a member of Phi Beta Kappa and is past chairman of the speaker's bureau of the National Conference of Christians and Jews.

HARRY A. ROBINSON

One of the top young men in public relations today is twenty-nine-year-old Harry Robinson, a onetime athlete, sports writer, copy editor and busboy. Currently, he is director of public relations for the National Conference of Christians and Jews, Inc., handling press relations, radio and television liaison, magazine contacts, research writing, the editing of news and the development of feature stories and scripts. The job also includes the supervision of photography and film, tape recordings and graphics. In short, he is in charge of general planning and execution of the conference's P.R. program.

This is a big responsibility, but Harry Robinson was prepared for it. His previous position was that of account executive for Harshe-Rotman & Druck, Inc., a large New York P.R. firm. Among his assignments at HR&D was that of developing a program for the United Negro College Fund that enabled it to obtain greater financial support for its thirty-six predominantly black schools. Part of the program involved setting up a Black Executive Committee, establishing contact with the White House and launching a publicity campaign aimed at influential people in public life.

Like many P.R. men, Robinson sharpened his skills as a newspaperman. After graduating from Rutgers University (he worked his way through as a busboy, waiter and delivery-man), he joined the *Newark News* as a sports writer and scholastic sports editor. A former athlete himself, he covered high school and college football, baseball, track, swimming, soccer, golf, tennis and even horseshoe pitching. During this time he also collaborated on a series of stories on black athletes for Newspaper Enterprise Association, a syndicated feature service. Robinson's newspaper work included a stint on the copy desk as a headline writer and makeup man, a job that consists of arranging the stories in the way they will appear in the published paper.

Robinson holds that the young man or woman planning a public relations career should keep in mind that it is "largely an intangible area."

"You will find," he continued, "that good old common sense and the ability to perceive troublesome situations and develop methods of circumventing them depends on the individual. One's appearance and the security of being able to communicate with a cross-section of people, yet at the same time commanding their respect, also is highly important."

According to Robinson, the required background for public relations is the same for all beginners, "white, black, brown, red or yellow."

"The first thing I would recommend," he said, "is to be a voracious reader. Read everything—newspapers, magazines and books. The amount of knowledge gleaned from reading is incredible. The majority of people who are considered extremely intelligent simply are knowledgeable about a variety of subjects and are thus able to discuss virtually anything that comes up.

"Additionally, reading permits you to develop a strong command of the language. Consequently, in writing you have a greater flexibility. You don't have to rely on colloquial, hackneyed terms."

The public-relations executive stressed the need to acquire strong writing habits and techniques. "A concise sentence which makes your point is always best," he said. "The ability to organize your thoughts and ideas and to smoothly develop them on paper is of the utmost importance."

Harry Robinson is one of a growing number of black professionals who earn enough to put them in the middle- or high-income bracket. His attitude toward his status was summed up in an interview with Ernest Johnston, Jr., of the *New York Post*.

"I wouldn't necessarily say that I'm middle-class in my views toward the racial problem in this country," Robinson said. "You might say that I'm quasi-militant. But as far as money is concerned, I'm middle-class."

However, his goal encompasses more than making money. His work for the National Conference of Christians and Jews puts him in constant touch with persons in religion, business, education and government, as well as with youths of all colors. The objectives: a better world in which people treat each other as human beings, not as members of a particular race.

BLACK AGENCIES

There are an estimated forty-five black advertising and public relations firms in the United States. A few are successful, some have moderate billings and still others are struggling to keep afloat. If they die there will undoubtedly be others to take their place. Black owners of ad and P.R. agencies believe they have a distinct advantage over their white counterparts. One such executive told *Black Enterprise* magazine:

"We can provide black creative talent with an outlet for their black experience, which is not true where blacks are working in white agencies. These blacks often turn into white Negroes creating white commercials."

Two of the most profitable black agencies are Vince Cullers Advertising, Inc., of Chicago, and New York City's Howard Sanders Advertising and Public Relations. Fifteen years ago, Cullers was believed to be the only black owner of an advertising agency. He got his start as a free-lance artist, finding closed doors at white agencies when he tried to get a staff job. His agency now has billings of more than a million dollars a year and represents both white and black advertisers. In 1968 Cullers shocked many whites with his Newport cigarette ad featuring a "black revolutionary" wearing a dashiki. Many of Cullers' print and radio ads are on behalf of clients who want to stress black pride, such as Johnson Products "Afro-Sheen" hair. One ad for the product carried the line: "A beautiful new product for a beautiful new people"— a far cry from the wording of older ads for cosmetics designed to bleach skin and straighten hair.

"Black separatism is a fact, and we deal with it in a positive way," Cullers said.

Howard Sanders is a former radio executive who opened his own agency on Madison Avenue in 1966 and is currently reputed to have billings of more than one and a half million dollars. His accounts include the R. J. Reynolds Tobacco Company and Pepsi Cola. Sanders got the idea for his own agency while a salesman for a black radio station. "I would often have to revise the entire advertising campaign written by the white agency because it was irrelevant to the black community," he recalled. One of his ads for R. J. Reynolds showed a black man in a white shirt and tie adjusting a complex piece of laboratory equipment. The caption: "What's Franklin Weaver doing in our chemical plant if he's not there to sweep?"

One of the fastest-rising public-relations firms is Seymour & Lundy Associates, Inc., of Detroit. Its founder and president, Frank M. Seymour, began his career as the educational director of Local 50 of the United Automobile Workers union in Ypsilanti, Michigan. Part of his duties included working on the union newspaper. He was the first black man elected to the Ypsilanti City Council, which has had a black councilman and/or mayor ever since. In 1945 he founded his own newspaper, *The Ypsilanti Voice*, which had a circulation of 28,000 when he sold it to his white partner. He then took on a series of public relations and broadcasting positions, becoming P.R. director of the Altes Brewing Company on the strength of his handling of the televising of the first black golf tournament. He first opened his own P.R. agency in Cleveland, but left it to work in radio. He founded his present firm in 1965.

Seymour said:

Public relations has long been thought of as a glamour occupation. Many young people—and even more adults —believe the workday of the public relations professional is immersed in rubbing elbows with celebrities, confabing with newspaper executives, making TV appearances, attending cocktail parties and little else.

To be sure, there have been so-called public relations men who fit all or part of this description. But the great majority of the *true professionals* happily fall outside this definition.

Before you seriously consider public relations as a career, make certain you know what it's all about! One definition says that public relations evaluates public attitudes, identifies the policies and procedures of an individual or an organization with the public interest and plans and executes a program of action to earn public understanding and acceptance. In other words, public relations forges a link of service and communication with the public. Not all public relations practitioners will agree with this definition totally. But most would agree with its spirit.

It should be noted here that public relations agencies are only one aspect of this field. Many organizations employ their own public-relations personnel. These include corporations, trade groups such as milk producers, charitable foundations, schools and colleges, hospitals, professional societies and governmental offices and departments. One of the biggest sources of these jobs is the United States government. The Defense Department alone has dozens of publicity men and women. Most of these experts first worked for magazines or newspapers, where they acquired or polished communication skills.

Still other P.R. assignments are in community relations rather than with the press. For example, a company that's moving its plant to a new town wants the cooperation and goodwill of the residents. Thus, the task of a public-relations man would be to ease the way for the new facility by assuring citizens that it will be good for their community by providing jobs and other benefits.

Sound journalistic skills will be of immense value in any phase of public relations. It must be remembered that the P.R. expert exists largely because of the mass media. His main task is to get his client's message to the public.

9 / Doing Your Own Thing

Some black students have told me that they have grave misgivings about working for the white media because they do not feel they will get the opportunity to do their own thing —that is, to tell the black story as they feel it should be told. These same students also question the standard of objectivity in reporting to which most Establishment newspapers and broadcast stations subscribe. The young blacks cannot reconcile their view of the white world and the history of their race in America with an obligation to be objective about news, especially racial news.

I have no all-embracing answer to these questions. I believe each person should decide for himself whether he wants to work for the white or black media. Certainly the satisfactions mentioned earlier can be found as readily on black newspapers, magazines and advertising agencies as on white ones —perhaps more so. The monetary reward is not likely to be as great, but that may not be one's primary reason for choosing a job.

However, there are black reporters, writers, etc., who are, to a great extent, doing their own thing in the white media. They are suggesting stories, usually about the black community, and being given the opportunity to investigate and write them for publication. Black television reporters do, in many instances, win arguments with assignment editors on what news to cover. And documentaries about blacks have been written, directed and produced by blacks.

This is not to say that all blacks in the white media are
happy or that they all get to do what they want to. Instances
of dissatisfaction and frustration have been documented in
this book. But it must be remembered that very few people in
the media have unlimited freedom of action. Newspaper,
magazine and broadcast reporters work under editors who
generally make the major editorial decisions and policies.
Sometimes they're right, and sometimes they're wrong; but
they are the people in charge. This fact is generally true for
public relations and advertising as well. Copywriters, artists,
junior account executives and other creative personnel report
to managers and senior executives. On newspapers especially,
the frustrations of reporters in coping with city editors
represent one of the oldest problems in journalism. More than
one idealistic young reporter has quit because he couldn't
cover the stories of his choice, or in the way he wanted to.

There are recent signs that the dictatorial control of editors is coming to an end or at least undergoing modification.
On the more progressive dailies, reporters are being given a
voice in editorial decision. A number of papers have adopted
team or task-force reporting in which from four to seven reporters are detached from regular duties to work on specific
assignments such as investigating slum conditions, police cor-
ruption or drug use and addiction. There also is more newspaper emphasis on social change, a concern for the environment, the playing down of crime news and the creation of
new specialists. These changes mean that reporters are being
given more freedom of movement and some say in policy.
The shifts are part of a process that began in the second half
of the 1960s in the wake of racial and campus revolution,
dramatic changes in American life styles, the awareness of
pollution, the war in Southeast Asia, urban decay and other
issues. Newspapers such as the *Milwaukee Journal*, the *Chi-*

cago Tribune, the *New York Daily News*, the *Wilmington News-Journal* and *The New York Times* are re-examining old reporting concepts and casting them aside if they don't fit today's needs.

This trend will not be reversed. Faced with powerful competition from magazines and television, newspapers must keep abreast of the times if they are to survive. A number of newspapers have folded in recent years, partly because they clung to old methods. Many papers are re-examining their methods to see if they fit the times. Objectivity is not being abandoned, but it is being given greater flexibility. There is, for example, a trend toward the analytical and interpretive story in which the writer backgrounds the facts in a way that they can be better understood.

Objectivity is not as confining as one may think. By simply reporting what he sees and uncovers, a newsman can accomplish a great deal toward improving social and economic conditions. What more needs to be added to a straight report of a slum neighborhood? The concerned reader will be moved without being harangued.

Objective or fair reporting means that when a person claims he was a victim of police brutality, the reporter gets his story and then asks the police if they care to reply. In other words, objectivity is simply fairness, a journalistic theory that, while not perfect, has made the American press one of the most reliable in the world. In many countries, the news media are government organs or the mouthpieces of political parties and cannot be depended upon for unbiased reporting. Even in nations where the government does not officially control the press, newspapers are so fearful of censorship and punishment that they peddle the government line anyway.

It must be said, of course, that the black population has

had good reason for misgivings about the press in the United States. For years the white media espoused a purely white point of view, spoke in a weak voice (or no voice) about racial wrongs and were slow to hire blacks for editorial jobs. It is slower still in appointing blacks to managerial and executive positions. But this is changing. The impetus and publicity given by the press to civil rights activities has done much to bring about change.

Blacks are playing increasingly important roles in the communications field—journalism, radio and television, advertising and public relations. Some of them have chosen to concentrate on black issues; others have not. But in almost every case, the black impact and opportunity are increasing, and there is every indication that they will continue to do so in the future.

Bibliography

American Journalism, A History, Frank Luther Mott, New York: Macmillan, 1962.

Before the Mayflower: A History of Black America, Lerone Bennett, Jr., Chicago: Johnson Publishing Co., Inc., 1969.

Black Press, The: A Bibliography, Armistead S. Pride, Madison, Wisconsin: Association for Education in Journalism, 1968.

Black Press, U.S.A., The, Roland E. Wolseley, Ames, Iowa: Iowa State University Press, 1971.

Broadcast News Careers, Radio-Television News Directors Association, Iowa City, Iowa: School of Journalism, University of Iowa.

Careers in Journalism, Quill and Scroll Foundation, Iowa City, Iowa: University of Iowa Press.

Depth Reporting: An Approach to Journalism, Neale Copple, Englewood Cliffs, N.J.: Prentice-Hall, Inc., 1964.

Freedom of the Press—A Continuing Struggle, M. L. Stein, New York: Julian Messner, 1966.

Go South to Sorrow, Carl T. Rowan, New York: Random House, 1957.

How I Got That Story, members of the Overseas Press Club of America, edited by David Brown and W. Richard Bruner, New York: E. P. Dutton & Co., 1967.

Introduction to Mass Communications, Edwin Emery, Phillip H. Ault and Warren Agee, New York: Dodd Mead, 1970 (third edition).

Journalism in a Free Society, Vern E. Edwards, Dubuque, Iowa: W. C. Brown Co., 1970.

Lonely Warrior, The: The Life and Times of Robert S. Abbott, Roi Ottley, Chicago: Henry Regnery Co., 1955.

Mass Media, The, William L. Rivers, New York: Harper & Row, 1964.

Media and the Cities, The, Charles U. Daly, editor, Chicago: University of Chicago Center for Policy Studies, 1968.

Negro in New York, The, edited by Roi Ottley and William J. Weatherby, Dobbs Ferry, New York: Oceana Publications, Inc., 1967.

Negro Newspaper, The, Vishnu V. Oak, Antioch, Ohio: Antioch Press, 1948.

News, The, Joan Murray, New York: McGraw-Hill, 1968.

Press and Its Problems, The, Curtis D. MacDougall, Dubuque, Iowa: W. C. Brown Co., 1964.

Professional Journalist, The, John Hohenberg, New York: Holt Rinehart and Winston, 1969 (second edition).

Race and the News Media, edited by Paul L. Fisher and Ralph L. Lowenstein, New York: Frederick A. Prager, 1967 (also in paper-back).

Reporting Today: The Newswriter's Handbook, M. L. Stein, New York: Cornerstone Library, 1971 (paperback).

Student Journalist, The, Edmund C. Arnold and Hillier Krieghbaum, New York: New York University Press, 1963.

Television News, Irving Fang, New York: Hastings House, 1968.

Television News Reporting, CBS News, New York: McGraw-Hill, 1958.

This Is Our War: Selected Stories of Six Afro-American War Correspondents, Baltimore: Afro-American Publishing Co., 1945.

Watch Your Language, Theodore M. Bernstein, Manhasset, N.Y.: Channel Press, 1958 (paperback).

Write Clearly . . . Speak Effectively, M. L. Stein, New York: Cornerstone Library, 1967 (paperback).

Your Career in Advertising, George Johnson, New York: Julian Messner, 1966.

Your Career in Journalism, M. L. Stein, New York: Julian Messner, 1965.

Your Career in Public Relations, Jody Donohue, New York: Julian Messner, 1967.

Your Career in TV and Radio, George N. Gordon and Irving A. Falk, New York: Julian Messner, 1969.

Sources of Further Information

Colleges and universities offering majors or programs in journalism, including newspaper work, magazine writing and editing, broadcast journalism, public relations and advertising.

AMERICAN ASSOCIATION OF SCHOOLS AND DEPARTMENTS OF JOURNALISM

University of Arizona, Tucson, Arizona 85710
*Boston University, Boston, Massachusetts 02215
*California State College, Fullerton, California 92631
*University of Colorado, Boulder, Colorado 80302
*Columbia University, New York, New York 10027
*University of Florida, Gainesville, Florida 32601
*Fresno State College, Fresno, California 93710
*University of Georgia, Athens, Georgia 30601
University of Houston, Houston, Texas 77004
*University of Illinois, Urbana, Illinois 61801
*Indiana University, Bloomington, Indiana 47401
*University of Iowa, Iowa City, Iowa 52240
*Iowa State University, Ames, Iowa 50010
*University of Kansas, Lawrence, Kansas 66044
*Kansas State University, Manhattan, Kansas 66502
*Kent State University, Kent, Ohio 44242
*University of Kentucky, Lexington, Kentucky 40506

* Denotes both undergraduate and graduate journalism programs.

*Louisiana State University, Baton Rouge, Louisiana 70803

*University of Maryland, College Park, Maryland 20742

*University of Michigan, Ann Arbor, Michigan 48103

*Michigan State University, East Lansing, Michigan 48823

*University of Minnesota, Minneapolis, Minnesota 55455

*University of Missouri, Columbia, Missouri 65201

*University of Montana, Missoula, Montana 59801

University of Nebraska, Lincoln, Nebraska 68508

*University of Nevada, Reno, Nevada 89507

University of New Mexico, Albuquerque, New Mexico 87106

New York University, New York, New York 10003

*University of North Carolina, Chapel Hill, North Carolina 27514

*Northern Illinois University, DeKalb, Illinois 60115

*North Texas State University, Denton, Texas 76203

*Northwestern University, Evanston, Illinois 60201

*Ohio State University, Columbus, Ohio 43210

*Ohio University, Athens, Ohio 45701

*Pennsylvania State University, University Park, Pennsylvania 16802

Rutgers University, New Brunswick, New Jersey 08903

*San Diego State College, San Diego, California 92115

*San Fernando Valley State College, Northridge, California 91324

San Francisco State College, San Francisco, California 94132

*San Jose State College, San Jose, California 95114

*Temple University, Philadelphia, Pennsylvania 19122

*University of South Carolina, Columbia, South Carolina 29208

*South Dakota State University, Brookings, South Dakota 57006

*University of Southern California, Los Angeles, California 90007
*Southern Illinois University, Carbondale, Illinois 62901
*Stanford University, Stanford, California 94305
*Syracuse University, Syracuse, New York 13210
*University of Tennessee, Knoxville, Tennessee 37916
*University of Texas, Austin, Texas 78712
 Texas A & M University, College Sta., Texas 77843
 Texas Christian University, Fort Worth, Texas 76129
*Texas Technological College, Lubbock, Texas 79409
*University of Utah, Salt Lake City, Utah 84112
*University of North Dakota, Grand Forks, North Dakota 58201
*University of Oklahoma, Norman, Oklahoma 73069
*Oklahoma State University, Stillwater, Oklahoma 74074
*University of Oregon, Eugene, Oregon 97403
*University of Washington, Seattle, Washington 98105
 Washington and Lee University, Lexington, Virginia 24450
*West Virginia University, Morgantown, West Virginia 26506
*University of Wisconsin, Madison, Wisconsin 53706

The above schools and departments of journalism are accredited in one or more sequences by the American Council on Education for Journalism.

AMERICAN SOCIETY OF JOURNALISM SCHOOL ADMINISTRATORS

*University of Alabama, Tuscaloosa, Alabama 35486
*American University, Washington, D.C. 20016
 Angelo State University, San Angelo, Texas 76901
*Arizona State University, Tempe, Arizona 85281

*Ball State University, Muncie, Indiana 47306

Baylor University, Waco, Texas 76703

Bradley University, Peoria, Illinois 61606

*University of Bridgeport, Bridgeport, Connecticut 06602

*Brigham Young University, Provo, Utah 84601

California State College, Hayward, California 94542

*California State College, Long Beach, California 90801

California State College, Los Angeles, California 90032

California State Polytechnic College, San Luis Obispo, California 93401

Chico State College, Chico, California 95926

*Colorado State University, Fort Collins, Colorado 80521

Creighton University, Omaha, Nebraska 68131

Drake University, Des Moines, Iowa 50311

Duquesne University, Pittsburgh, Pennsylvania 15219

*East Texas State University, Commerce, Texas 75428

Fordham University, Bronx, New York 10458

*Fresno State College, Fresno, California 93710

*George Washington University, Washington, D.C. 20006

Georgia State University, Atlanta, Georgia 30303

Idaho State University, Pocatello, Idaho 83201

University of Idaho, Moscow, Idaho 83843

*Kent State University, Kent, Ohio 44242

Lincoln University, Jefferson City, Missouri 65101

Long Island University, Brooklyn, New York 11201

University of Maine, Orono, Maine 04473

*Marshall University, Huntington, West Virginia 25701

*University of Maryland, College Park, Maryland 20742

University of Massachusetts, Amherst, Massachusetts 01002

Memphis State University, Memphis, Tennessee 38111

University of Miami, Coral Gables, Florida 33124

*Mississippi State Women's College, Columbus, Mississippi 39701

*University of Mississippi, University, Mississippi 38677
Moorhead State College, Moorhead, Minnesota 56560
*Murray State University, Murray, Kentucky 42071
University of Nebraska, Omaha, Nebraska 68101
*University of Nevada, Reno, Nevada 89507
New Mexico State University, Las Cruces, New Mexico 88001
New York University, New York, New York 10003
*University of North Dakota, Grand Forks, North Dakota 58201
*North Texas State University, Denton, Texas 76203
*Northern Illinois University, DeKalb, Illinois 60115
Ohio Wesleyan University, Delaware, Ohio 43015
*Oklahoma State University, Stillwater, Oklahoma 74074
Oregon State University, Corvallis, Oregon 97331
University of Rhode Island, Kingston, Rhode Island 02881
Sacramento State College, Sacramento, California 95819
St. Bonaventure University, St. Bonaventure, New York 14778
College of St. Thomas, St. Paul, Minnesota 55101
Samford University, Birmingham, Alabama 35209
San Francisco State College, San Francisco, California 94132
*San Jose State College, San Jose, California 95114
*University of South Carolina, Columbia, South Carolina 29208
*University of Southern California, Los Angeles, California 90007
*Southern Illinois University, Carbondale, Illinois 62901
Southern Methodist University, Dallas, Texas 75222
Southwest Texas State College, San Marcos, Texas 78666
*Temple University, Philadelphia, Pennsylvania 19122
Texas A & I University, Kingsville, Texas 78363

Texas A & M University, College Station, Texas 77843

Texas Christian University, Fort Worth, Texas 76129

°Texas Tech University, Lubbock, Texas 79409

Texas Woman's University, Denton, Texas 76105

University of Toledo, Toledo, Ohio 43606

°University of Tulsa, Tulsa, Oklahoma 74104

Utah State University, Logan, Utah 84321

°University of Utah, Salt Lake City, Utah 84112

Washington State University, Pullman, Washington 99163

Wayne State University, Detroit, Michigan 48202

°West Virginia University, Morgantown, West Virginia 25606

Wichita State University, Wichita, Kansas 67208

Wisconsin State University, Eau Claire, Wisconsin 54701

Wisconsin State University, Oshkosh, Wisconsin 54901

°University of Wyoming, Laramie, Wyoming 82070

PREDOMINATELY BLACK COLLEGES AND UNIVERSITIES OFFERING ONE OR MORE JOURNALISM COURSES

Alabama State University, Montgomery, Alabama 36101

Albany State College, Albany, Georgia 31705

Bennett College, Greensboro, North Carolina 27420

Bishop College, Dallas, Texas 75421

Central State College, Edmond, Oklahoma 73034

Clark College, Atlanta, Georgia 30314

Delaware State College, Dover, Delaware 19901

Elizabeth City State University, Elizabeth City, North Carolina 27909

Florida Memorial College, Miami, Florida 33054

Fort Valley State College, Fort Valley, Georgia 31030

Grambling College, Grambling, Louisiana 71245

Hampton Institute, Hampton, Virginia 23368

Howard University, Washington, D.C. 20001

Huston-Tillotson College, Austin, Texas 78702

Jackson State College, Jackson, Mississippi 39217

Johnson C. Smith University, Charlotte, North Carolina
28208

Kentucky State College, Frankfort, Kentucky 40601

Langston University, Langston, Oklahoma 73050

Lincoln University (Mo.), Jefferson City, Missouri 65101

Lincoln University (Pa.), Lincoln, Pennsylvania 19352

Livingstone College, Salisbury, North Carolina 28144

Malcolm X College, Chicago, Illinois

Mississippi Valley State College, Itta Bena, Mississippi 38941

Morgan State College, Baltimore, Maryland 21212

Morris Brown College, Atlanta, Georgia 30314

Norfolk State College, Norfolk, Virginia 23504

North Carolina A & T State University, Greensboro, North
Carolina 27411

North Carolina Central University, Durham, North Carolina
27707

Oakwood College, Huntsville, Alabama 35806

Philander Smith College, Little Rock, Arkansas 72203

St. Augustine's College, Raleigh, North Carolina 27602

Savannah State College, Savannah, Georgia 31404

Shaw University, Raleigh, North Carolina 27602

Tennessee A & I State University, Nashville, Tennessee 37203

Texas Southern University, Houston, Texas 77004

Tuskagee Institute, Tuskagee, Alabama 36088

Virginia Union College, Richmond, Virginia 23220

Virginia State College, Petersburg, Virginia 23803

Winston-Salem State University, Winston-Salem, North Carolina 27102

Xavier University, New Orleans, Louisiana 70125

Index

About the Author

While still in junior high school, M. L. Stein, a native of Escanaba, Michigan, decided to be a newspaperman. He prepared for his career by majoring in journalism at the University of Missouri. During Army service he contributed short stories to *Yank* and was a part-time correspondent for *Stars & Stripes*. After the war, he got his first job with the Royal Oak (Michigan) *Daily Tribune*. He has also been a reporter for the San Francisco *Examiner*, and *Time*, *Life* and *Fortune* magazines, and has written several books and many magazine articles. Mr. Stein and his family live in Port Washington, New York, and he commutes from there to New York University where he is chairman of the Department of Journalism.